Crypto Inv

In 2021

The Ultimate Guide To Gain Money From Holding Bitcoin And Exploiting The Altcoin Season. | Including 9 Projects With HUGE Profit Potential

David Smith Jr

Table of Contents

Introduction

The global economy is heavily dependent on digital methods of payment. The Trade in the context of e-commerce needs, for example, the use of digital tokens. The payment methods in the digital currency system are the string of bits. It presents a problem since, like every other digital archive, these bits' strings can quickly be replicated & reused for payment. By utilizing it twice, which is termed the double-spending problem, that digital token may be falsified. This issue has historically been resolved by focusing on a trustworthy third party who maintains a consolidated ledger for a charge & moves balances by crediting & debiting buyers & sellers' accounts. Such third party is also the provider of digital money itself, with PayPal being the famous example, & the popularity of currency comes from the assumption that consumers trust that the third party forbids double spending.

Cryptocurrencies like Bitcoin go quite a leap further & eliminate the third party's requirement that is trusted. Rather, to preserve & upgrade copies of the ledge, they depend on a decentralized network of (potentially anonymous) validators. This ensures that trust is preserved between validators on the right record of the transactions such that consumers can be confident of obtaining & retaining control of the balances. Finally, such consensus demands that (I) users should not double-spend currency & (ii) also that users could trust validators to change the ledger correctly. Why are cryptocurrencies like Bitcoin handling these challenges? Confidence in the cryptocurrency is focused on the blockchain that guarantees the transaction histories' distributed database is checked, updated & stored. This is achieved by setting up a blockchain. The block is indeed a series of transactions carried out among users of the cryptocurrency. From all of these blocks, the chain is generated with the background of previous transactions that enables one to build a ledger in which the sum of balances/currency a user owns can be checked publicly.

The cryptocurrency market has become a decentralized virtual currency network, which indicates that it runs independently of a central server via peer-to-peer transaction testing. The transactions are applied to the blockchain, a shared database ledger that stores details through 'mining' when the cryptocurrencies are acquired & sold.

Cryptocurrencies are often popularly volatile, making it necessary to consider when the sector is going to move, from the ICOs & blockchain forks to the breaking news and government regulation.

Consequently, the blockchain is just like a document that holds all prior transactions in the ledger, with the block becoming a fresh page that documents all existing transactions. Such competition will take different forms. It exists in Bitcoin via a procedure called mining. The Miners (or transaction validators) are competing to solve a costly computational challenge called the proof of the work (PoW). The winners of such a mining method are entitled to update the new block of the chain. Its consensus protocol then recommends that the "longest" past be known as the trustworthy public record. Because authentication & mining of transactions are expensive, an incentive mechanism is necessary for the mining to occur. For example, in Bitcoin, certain incentives are presently financed through fresh coins & transaction fees. The double-spending dilemma is the key issue among consumers.

In contrast, the trusting of a cryptocurrency: upon carrying out a transaction, a consumer tries to persuade the validators (& thus the general public whether blockchain is supported) to accept an alternate background under which any payment is carried out. The likelihood of this double spending will, thus, weaken trust in cryptocurrency. Naturally, a blockchain built on the PoW consensus protocol struggles with shifting backward transaction records. Consequently, whenever an entity wants to undo a transaction within the past, the person would suggest an alternate blockchain (with the specific transaction removed) & execute the PoW on any newly proposed blocks. Blockchain must be dynamically stable in that existing transactions should be connected to the transactions in all of the previous blocks. Redoing the past of the transactions backward is also very expensive if the portion of the chain that has to be substituted is long. Therefore, the more people will believe them, the "older" transactions were. Regrettably, a blockchain doesn't immediately safeguard a cryptocurrency from a forward-looking double-pending attack. The purchaser instructs a miner to pass a deposit to the supplier, whereas the seller produces the products concurrently. Note that perhaps the buyer may still mine the alternate history secretly (or apply a separate history to other miners) where the money is not passed. The transaction's final result relies on the payment instruction that is first inserted into the blockchain. Double-spending effort fails if the previous payment directive is added. The seller collects the payment & the buyer purchases the items. The double-spending effort works if the other is embraced instead. In this scenario, despite paying the seller, the consumer gets goods. By inserting confirmation lag into purchases, even double-spending assault may be prevented. It becomes more difficult to change transactions in a set of blocks by waiting for certain blocks before finishing the contract (e.g., seller prevents the arrival of goods).

With one new block, the vendor provides the products only when the payment is integrated into the blockchain. Once more, a possible history under which the transaction does not exist may be illegally mined by the buyer. Depending on the mining market and the duration of confirmation lag, how effectively hidden mining is. Assume the buyer fixes PoW for block representing the alternate history efficiently. Notice that buyers can either instantly broadcast the privately mined block or withhold it for potential mining. The seller will then not collect payment if he decides to broadcast block instantly, but he'll also not supply the product. Thus, for the buyer, double-spending assault is not effective.

Conversely, the buyer may withhold the block resolved temporarily & begin to mine another block privately. In particular, to persuade the seller to supply the goods, the buyer has to enable some miners to validate the seller's initial payment. Around the same moment, two blocks in a row with which the initial transaction is excluded must be privately mined by the buyer. If the buyer successfully mines two blocks quicker than most miners, he will reveal an alternate blockchain once the items are shipped.

Throughout this scenario, despite paying the seller, the consumer gets goods. More commonly, if the seller receives the products just after obtaining payment confirmations and double expenditure effectively, the buyer must overcome blocks N+ 1 times consecutively.

To sum up, confidence in a cryptocurrency framework includes the interaction of three concepts: blockchain security, mining environment health, & currency value. Appropriate mining operations are needed to maintain the blockchain's security, defend it from assaults and fraudulent behaviors. Besides, cryptocurrency would be generally adopted and exchanged at high valuation only when consumers trust the system's protection. Eventually, currency valuation helps the incentive system allow miners to invest in expensive mining operations.

The distinguishing characteristic of the cryptocurrency is that no other central authority is issued, making it potentially resistant to the government's direct intervention or coercion. To define cryptocurrency threats, features of the network (i.e., Blockchain) on which the cryptocurrency is centered must first be recognized. For all cryptocurrency transactions, the Blockchain is the digitized, decentralized, public ledger. It enables market players to record the digital currency transactions with no need for central recordkeeping as 'completed' blocks (most current transactions) are registered and applied to it in sequential order.

Each node (a network-connected computer) receives a copy of the blockchain, which is immediately downloaded.

Several nations also deem cryptocurrencies unconstitutional and either have outlawed them or who have trade and usage limits. There are the four most prominent nations in which cryptocurrencies have also been prohibited or rendered outright unlawful.

In this book, you will learn all the basics of cryptocurrency, its benefits, and risks. You will also learn how it works and the types of different cryptocurrencies presently available. You will also learn about cryptocurrency exchange and cryptocurrency exchange software—some tips on cryptocurrency investment and management. We have also discussed cryptocurrency asset management, spoofing, coin burning and the future of the cryptocurrency in this book. Let's start with the basics.

Chapter 1: Basics of Cryptocurrency

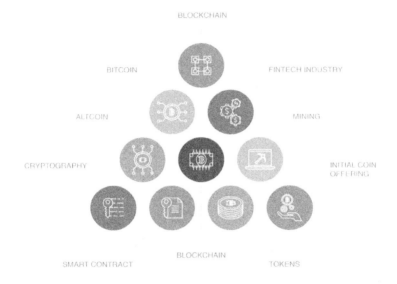

Cryptocurrency is anything from the money of the future to an incredibly volatile commodity that a ten-foot pole cannot reach. What is it, then? So, this is the major question: should you be spending on it?

Cryptocurrency innovations and tactics are spreading quickly. This is since a complex and special technology that is also available is cryptocurrencies. I say that, regardless of context, it can be grasped by everybody, which is how it keeps spreading.

Let's not ignore all cryptocurrency FOMO (fear of losing out) it offers. Maybe later, you've had it.

It feels like something significant occurs every week in the cryptocurrency business, from Bitcoin reaching major valuation peaks to Facebook releasing their multinational cryptocurrency, conversations on the effects of the cryptocurrency community, and dramatic price rises and crashes.

This will leave you questioning if you can invest in it, whether it's even secure, or how it operates.

This book would do that: start with understanding the fundamentals of cryptocurrency by breaking down its complicated essence so that you will become even more informed about the topic. You should give a decision over your investment needs only once you grasp these fundamentals.

You would have an overview of cryptocurrency fundamentals by the end of the chapter, such as:

- What is cryptocurrency is?

- The numerous crypto-currency forms

- The proposed laws and the law around them

- How it is purchased and sold by investors

- Investors adopted best practices.

1.1. What Is Cryptocurrency?

It's quick to get snapped over cryptocurrency technicalities, but let's begin with the cryptocurrency fundamentals. Cryptocurrency is money in digital form. There are no actual coins or bills attached to something that's purely digital.

They are not connected to the valuable assets; these are not linked in the material realm to something of importance, & this helps the value you have probably seen fluctuate erratically.

For example, in July 2019, after being fairly constant for a day, Bitcoin dropped around $530, or 5 percent, in an around 40-minute period. Why? Speculation persisted, but no real answers. Cryptocurrencies have little usage or worth outside of ownership, unlike securities, stocks, real estate, artwork, or precious metals.

The creator of GoldSilver, Mike Maloney, tends to equate crypto with gold, except for the major difference that gold has a meaning outside of being used for currencies.

In electronics & jewelry, gold is a critical factor and has importance outside of its small availability.

On the other side, bitcoin costs money because someone

else would have it & needs money to transfer it to you.

Two challenges, in general, have already been faced by currencies:

- To rule their worth, output, and validity, they need a central authority.

- They fall prey to fraudulent growth.

To counter these particular concerns, Bitcoin, one of the several types of cryptocurrency, was created.

Both concerns are resolved by blockchain technology (which we'll discuss in a minute) & high-level encryption.

The system does not need a central authority to control it (in reality, it can't be regulated) since Bitcoin is automated & heavily encrypted, & transactions can't be fraudulent.

Response to the question, "what will it take to build a virtual currency without the need for a central authority?" that's all that bitcoin is."

1.2. Cryptocurrency Basics

You must indeed consider the following concepts and values to understand cryptocurrencies better:

1.2.1. Cryptography

Cryptocurrency uses cryptography to guarantee user accounts' confidentiality, and transfers are performed securely, the process of concealing and disclosing information.

1.2.2. Blockchain

The blockchain is kind of the Distributed Ledger Technology that is a multi-operator database (including nodes, computing devices)

This is a technology that governs an entire cryptocurrency. It's a computer database checking funds, balances, & transfers.

There are numerous blockchain applications for outside financial reasons, like supply chain management, art ownership tracking, & even digital collectibles.

A blockchain-related concept that'll also be included in the chapter is a node. The particular component of a larger data system in a blockchain is a node. The whole system will break apart without the nodes.

Cryptography & blockchain help generate new coins, execute legal transfers, & create a stable infrastructure for cryptocurrencies.

1.2.3. De-Centralized

Much like with Bitcoin, decentralization suggests that all authority control is spread to all peers on the network, & there is not one specific point of the failure.

For, e.g., anyone will need to access at least 51 percent of the vast network of the computers responsible for managing Bitcoin, which is deemed an impossible task to "hack" the Bitcoin.

1.2.4. Peer-to-Peer

Without the need for a broker, cryptocurrency could be sent directly between the two individuals. Such transactions are carried out with very low transmission costs, which compensate for the network, allowing consumers to circumvent high transaction fees through more conventional money transfer systems, which means that you don't need PayPal, Zelle, or even a bank.

1.3. The Different forms of the Cryptocurrencies

Since most individuals consider a cryptocurrency, they are likely to think about Bitcoin (BTC). It is a crypto-currency flagship, and this cryptocurrency spawned thousands of coins.

There are around 2,500 cryptocurrencies. All of them have their unique blockchain built to their requirements.

Do not even worry; to comprehend the cryptocurrency fundamentals, you shouldn't need to understand every cryptocurrency. To offer you the idea, let us just go through a couple of more popular types.

1.3.1 Bitcoin (BTC)

Bitcoin, which launched in 2009, had reigned as the king of all the other cryptocurrencies. It is referred to as the "digital gold" or cryptocurrency gold standard. It has nearly $240 billion in market capitalization. It still controls most cryptocurrencies with about a 70 trillion lion's share of the entire market cap.

Compared to the other financial instruments, trading in only a single Bitcoin is a pricey undertaking. One bitcoin is equal to $8,596.21, only, for instance.

1.3.2. Litecoin (LTC)

Litecoin was established as the fork (or the split) from Bitcoin & launched as competition in 2011, refers to as "silver to the Bitcoins gold."

The Litecoin was rendered to process the transactions quicker and easier as compared to Bitcoin.

1.3.3. Ethereum (ETH)

Another cryptocurrency giant is Ethereum, although it's not supposed to be the peer-to-peer financial payment in the same manner as Bitcoin is.

As the decentralized software framework which controls the smart contracts (procedurally executed contracts) & distributed apps ("decentralized" apps/ dApps that we will explore after that), Ethereum was introduced in 2015.

1.3.4. dApps

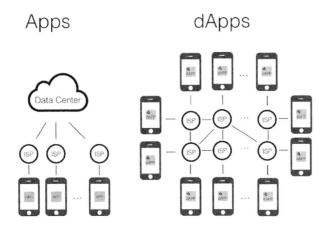

These decentralized apps are open source, independent, have 100percent annual uptime & gain from all the advantages of the blockchain (there is no central server, it is very difficult to hack, etc.)

Rather than being centralized by Apple, assume the applications in the iTunes store will be their entities. This is what the dApp is.

Using the blockchain of the Ethereum & the few Ethereum rivals' blockchains, including EOS, NEO, & Qtum, there are about 3,000 dapps.

1.3.5. Smart Contracts

These are the code strings that, when particular requirements are met, immediately perform a certain operation. For instance, by December 8, 2021, Alex might set up the smart contract to "pay Steven around $40 if he sends 10 of the unique logo designs."

If Steven does this assignment, a smart contract immediately costs him around $40. If he's not, otherwise Alex will get the $40 back.

1.4. Different Types of the Cryptocurrency

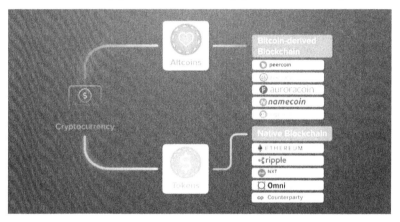

Let's go through a slight variation that, while attempting to learn the fundamentals of cryptocurrencies, often people are tripped over. There are two distinct cryptocurrency types: coins & tokens.

1.4.1. Coins

The coin is a type of cryptocurrency that, such as Bitcoin, Litecoin, Ripple, Ethereum, with its blockchain.

1.4.2. Token

The token is the type of cryptocurrency created on another blockchain, like Ethereum running on dApp. The tokens reflect a commodity or utility for a single project & are sold/ given to the Initial Coin Offerin, which mirrors the Initial Public Offering on the stock market during the 1st public sale. The United States government has concentrated on hunting down fake ICOs, but this is something we will learn later. For tokens, there is also another rather significant difference. Two general forms of tokens exist utility & security.

1.4.2.1. Utility token

A utility token is meant to be used only to purchase products that the business or network provides.

1.4.2.2. Security Token

The security token is a financial security digital version that serves as a share of just an enterprise's value, equivalent to how possessing AAPL implies owning a chunk of Apple.

In other terms, to create value for token holders, security tokens pay the dividends, distribute profits, pay interest, and invest in many other tokens or assets.

If it satisfies three conditions, a digital asset is called a security token.

- The monetary investment is needed.

- The funding collected goes to the specific enterprise.

- The Investors offer their capital intending to receive revenue from a third party's work.

Often, authentication tokens must be completely compatible & comply with all these regulations:

Regulation D: The person providing the security may only collect capital from certified investors, & then Free from the false or misleading statements must be given to them (Section 506C).

Regulation A+: Exception requires the developer to seek up to around $50 million in the investment from the non-accredited investors for the SEC-approved security. This choice requires a lot of time and seems to be normally the costliest issuance route.

Regulation S: This type of Regulation sets out security offers from the countries outside the United States who are not, however, subject to Section 5 of the 1993 Act for the registration. The creators of protection offerings must also comply with the nation's security laws they hope to seek investment.

A Cryptocurrency Transaction: Example

Here's how a hypothetical cryptocurrency exchange takes place to help grasp cryptocurrency fundamentals.

Let's say Alex needs to give $5 worth of the BTC to Steven.

1. Steven is giving Alex his Bitcoin address (known as the "hashed public key"). Any exchange or the cryptocurrency wallet set up by Steven is connected to this Bitcoin address. This is what appears like 3D94LKmtQuVG8JFB3F7cB7gwj614yG4CPg.

2. Within his cryptocurrency exchange/wallet, Alex inserts the address and sum of Bitcoin (BTC)-about 0.0005 BTC, which would be equal to over $5, & presses submit.

3. Steven pays a nominal charge without the BTC. These payments will vary anywhere from $ 0.05 to be shipped within the next hour or around $ 0.58 within 10 minutes, as per bitcoinfees.info. If Alex submitted $5 or around

$5,000,000, it doesn't matter, and the fees should both be the same.

How is this possible? But let us jump behind the scenes,

Any node in the Bitcoin network got a transaction request when Alex submitted a transaction to the blockchain. Any node guarantees that:

1. In reality, Alex is who he claims to be. The nodes check the identification of Alex via his secret key; your source of funds is marked through a private key. Entry to the money is open to anyone that has entry towards this private key. That's why making sure to hold the private key safe receives paramount importance.

2. He has $5 to give to Steven. Because the nodes have such a copy of the entire transaction ledger, they can easily verify if Alex does have money.

That transaction then goes through & nodes change ledger with the latest transaction if around 51 percent of nodes agree on two of the above items.

1.5. How Investors Buy or Trade Cryptocurrency?

In the past year, cryptocurrency purchasing has been a user-friendly procedure, with famous financial companies like Robinhood & Square Cash getting on the board.

Here are some alternate forms investors prefer currently buying or selling cryptocurrency to further raise the IQ of cryptocurrency.

1.5.1 Coinbase

Coinbase established its credibility as the pioneer in cryptocurrency trading room by radically simplifying the procedure of how users acquire cryptocurrencies.

Coinbase offers many of the largest trading rates out of cryptocurrency exchanges, including a 1.49 percent conversion rate while utilizing the bank account or the colossal 3.99 percent while using the credit card.

1.5.2 Coinbase Pro

Formerly identified as the GDAX, Coinbase Pro is an offering for even more intermediate users through Coinbase catering. Along with more trading tools, Coinbase Pro has much more sophisticated yet informative trading maps & graphs.

It is worth mentioning the processing fees: they vary from $0.10 to around $0.30 based on the order's size.

1.5.3 Binance

Binance is now one of the leading volume and consumer exchanges of cryptocurrencies.

Binance provides hundreds of various coins, sophisticated functionality for trading, plus robust maps & graphs for trading. Binance pays a 0.1 percent trading fee.

1.6. The Cryptocurrency Regulation & Rules

Your understanding of regulation will determine the opinions on the whole cryptocurrency.

Financial regulation is the consequence of catastrophic financial losses as well as illegal trade. Regulation is the result of the world's great depressions.

To prevent major losses, capital markets nowadays, such as public securities, are carefully regulated.

Cryptocurrencies, but on the other side, are not regulated.

In terms of cryptocurrencies, what the United States government has centered against has been people who launder money or purchase illicit drugs & utilities via cryptocurrency and detect fake ICOs & collect taxes.

Notice 2014-21 released by IRS is probably the most significant & crucial component of regulatory clarification for ordinary cryptocurrency users.

Notice 2014-21 states that cryptocurrency is regarded as property & comes under the general tax principles for federal tax purposes.

Therefore, if a single cryptocurrency is traded or used to buy items, utilities, and other cryptocurrencies, a benefit/loss must be acknowledged (such as trading Bitcoin for the Ethereum).

It's crucial to note that the legislative environment surrounding cryptocurrencies is in a state of change, with a couple of the biggest & most important milestone decisions already ahead among us. Some of them look into the fundamentals of cryptocurrency.

1.7. Cryptocurrency Best Practices

Although cryptocurrency enables everyone to be a bank on their own, certain harsh realities still come with all of this.

No central bank implies no customer support, no fixed wealth protection or the cryptocurrency sum FDIC insurance, and no representative to query when things go bad.

This leaves a significant danger to the cryptocurrency:

• Hacking from hostile third parties.

It is being lost through personal error, like giving the incorrect address to bitcoin or forgetting the private key.

Even then, when adopting blockchain best practices, all of these very concrete risks can be prevented.

The principles of cryptocurrency & encryption hygiene revolve around maintaining the private key secure.

Know, full access to the cryptocurrency is the private key. If you have written down the 64-character secret key on even a notecard & anyone has exposure to it, they will effectively transfer the cryptocurrency anywhere they wish.

Here is another short security checklist of cryptocurrencies that investors need.

1.8. Use Cryptocurrency Wallet

The cryptocurrency wallet is the platform that enables cryptocurrency to be stored, received, and then sent.

There are several various styles of wallets; however, hot& cold are mainly two categories.

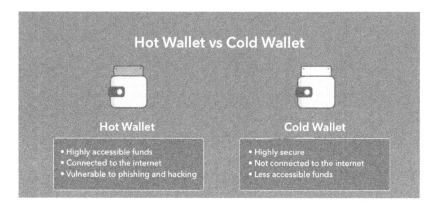

1.8.1 The Hot Wallets

The "Hot" wallets are related to the Internet in a way. Most cryptocurrency exchanges, for instance, even have a wallet function for users.

When a hacker can find his way through someone's trading account, cryptocurrency will be transferable. Furthermore, if the exchange itself is compromised, the criminals will even rob cryptocurrency.

A software wallet hosted on the computer as just an application is another common sort of hot wallet.

1.8.2. Cold Wallet

The "Cold" wallets are not connected to Internet & are thus more stable than the hot wallets theoretically. Many of the cryptocurrency exchanges containing large sums of cryptocurrency, for instance, prefer to store much of cryptocurrency in the offline cold wallets to mitigate the harm if there was a breach.

The Cold wallets have hardware wallets that are essentially tiny plastic machines built exclusively to hold the private key secure for anyone.

The paper wallet, which is the private key printed on a sheet of paper, is another common cold wallet.

The Two-Factor Verification Allowing (& Google Authenticator)

Note, in the context that anyone can control their code whenever they like, certain cryptocurrencies like Bitcoin could not be "hacked."

The positions that hold private keys, though, are very close to being compromised.

Someone's account is the first line of the defense. It is essential to be using safe & distinctive passwords that are not being used by any other account when funds are stored on the cryptocurrency exchange.

Enabling the two-factor authentication is the next move (2FA). If 2FA is allowed, they would also need to be accepted with the text sent to a person's password, even if somebody uses somebody else's password.

When available, another extra layer of protection is the Google Authenticator.

Google Authenticator is a phone app that conducts the 2FA authentication and produces fresh codes inserted correctly per 30 seconds to obtain entry to the account.

1.9. The Secret Is Education

Understanding the fundamentals of cryptocurrencies can allow one to be informed of the current debate around cryptocurrency that takes place anywhere.

Even you are deeply opposed to cryptocurrency. As just an

enthusiast, it is necessary not just to stay up with news, but also to clarify that to others, like friends & relatives, who might suggest putting money in it to understand it first.

In the end, it is the financial education that will aid in deciphering between the latest (& dangerous) trends vs. maximizing the returns with time through wise investment.

Chapter 2: Benefits of the Cryptocurrency

Major Benefits of cryptocurrency trading includes:

2.1. Cryptocurrency volatility

While the cryptocurrency industry is relatively young, it has encountered considerable volatility due to massive volumes of short-term trading activity. For, e.g., bitcoin prices grew as high as around $19,378 between October 2017 & October 2018 & dropped to the lows of $5851. Many cryptocurrencies have become relatively more secure, yet it is also possible that emerging developments would draw speculative attention.

Cryptocurrency uncertainty is part of what makes this business so thrilling. Rapid intraday market swings may provide traders with a variety of options to go for long & short, often with added danger. Whenever you intend to explore the demand for cryptocurrencies, make sure you carried out the research and made a risk management strategy.

2.2. Cryptocurrency market hours

The market for cryptocurrencies is commonly open to selling 24 hours per day, seven days a week, with no centralized market governance. Cryptocurrency transactions take place on cryptocurrency exchanges worldwide, directly amongst individuals. Even then, as the industry is transitioning to the infrastructural updates/ 'forks,' there could be downtime periods.

Through IG, around 4 am Saturday to around 10 pm on Friday (GMT), you will exchange cryptocurrencies with fiat currencies, including US dollars.

2.3. Improved liquidity

Liquidity is the indicator of how readily and efficiently a cryptocurrency, without changing the market price, may be exchanged into cash. Liquidity is critical because it brings in improved prices, quicker processing times, and enhanced precision for technological analysis.

In general, since trades are distributed through several markets, the cryptocurrency industry is called illiquid, which implies that relatively tiny transactions may significantly affect market values. This is part of the explanation why prices for cryptocurrencies are so unpredictable.

However, you will get increased liquidity when you exchange the cryptocurrency CFDs with the IG since we procure rates on your part from many venues. This suggests that the trades are much more probable to be completed at a cheaper cost & rapidly.

2.4. The capability to go long or go short.

If you acquire a cryptocurrency, you buy assets upfront with the expectation that value would improve. So, when you invest in the cryptocurrency's price, you will take advantage of stocks that are both dropping and - in price. This is referring to as going short.

2.5. The Short Selling or Going long

For instance, let's assume that since you think that the market will crash, you have chosen to open the short CFD place on the ether's price. If you were correct, & the value of ether dropped against the U.S. dollar, it will help your exchange. Conversely, if ether increases against the US dollar, a loss will be made from your place.

2.6. Leveraged exposure.

As the CFD trading is indeed a leveraged commodity, it helps to open the 'margin' position that is a deposit worth only the fraction of trade's maximum value. In other terms, although only locking up a comparatively limited sum of the money, you might obtain broad exposure to the cryptocurrency industry.

When it is closed, the benefit or loss that you gain on the cryptocurrency transactions will represent the maximum valuation of the position but selling on margin allows you the potential to make big gains on a comparatively small investment. However, it may even exacerbate any losses, even losses that with an individual transaction may outweigh your original deposit. That is why, before selling CFDs, it is important to recognize the overall worth of leveraged role.

Therefore, it is important to ensure that one must have an effective plan for risk control in effect, which can involve appropriate stops & limitations.

2.7. Faster account opening

You would need to purchase & sell cryptocurrencies from exchange once you buy them, which allows you to build

an exchange account & hold your cryptocurrency in a personal digital wallet. It may be restricting & time-consuming for this method.

But you won't involve links to exchange explicitly while dealing cryptocurrencies with the IG since we are accessible on your behalf to the underlying market. You will not need an exchange account & controlled, meaning you will be set up & ready to sell even sooner. Easy application form & instant online verification, by which you may be trading in much less than 5 minutes.

Chapter 3: The Risks of the Cryptocurrency

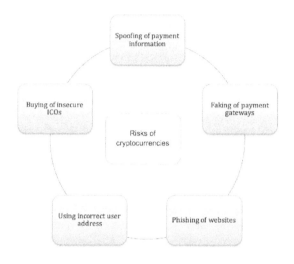

The distinguishing characteristic of the cryptocurrency is that no other central authority is issued, making it potentially resistant to the government's direct intervention or coercion. To define cryptocurrency threats, features of the network (i.e., Blockchain) on which the cryptocurrency is centered must first be recognized. For all cryptocurrency transactions, the Blockchain is the digitized, decentralized, public ledger. It enables market players to record the digital currency transactions with no need for central recordkeeping as 'completed' blocks (most current transactions) are registered and applied to it in sequential order. Each node (a network-connected computer) receives a copy of the blockchain, which is immediately downloaded.

Any of the challenges which cryptocurrencies face, such as the fact that a machine crash would delete one's digital wealth or that a hacker may ransack a digital bank, may be solved in the future through technological developments.

What would be more challenging to solve is the underlying phenomenon that cripples cryptocurrencies. The more successful they get, the more legislative and political attention they will expect to draw, eroding their creation's basic principle.

While the number of merchants embracing cryptocurrencies has risen slowly, they remain clearly in the small group. They must first achieve general recognition among users of cryptocurrencies to being even more widely used. Nevertheless, except for the electronically adept, their relative difficulty compared to the traditional currencies would discourage most individuals.

Nevertheless, with a straightforward description of where the digital currencies are and how the descendants will reach them if they do not take appropriate measures, you may set the immediate family for trouble with the law.

Preferably, that investors would regard both technological usability and ethical implications. Shareholders may establish their descendants for protracted litigation without addressing the legal questions involved with financial planning. On the other side, Morgan admits, "excluding [crypto] keys, the court order is powerless."

Nevertheless, with a straightforward description of where the digital currencies are and how the descendants will reach them if they do not take appropriate measures, you may set the immediate family for trouble with the law. Preferably, that investors would regard both technological usability and ethical implications. Shareholders may establish their descendants for protracted litigation without addressing the legal questions involved with financial planning. On the other side, Morgan admits, "excluding [crypto] keys, the court order is powerless."

The following risks refer to this technology platform.

Irreversible: A transaction can't be undone until confirmation; there is also no safety net.

Anonymous: There are no transactions or accounts related to real-world names; everything is digitalized through internet access.

Global Speed: Transactions on the network are almost automatic and then are validated in a few minutes. Because they exist in a vast network of computers, the physical position is oblivious. For authentication or confirmation, there are no outside parties involved.

Secure: Solid cryptography & the magic of large numbers render this scheme difficult to hack.

No Gatekeeper: The app that anyone will use is free of charge. You will accept & transfer Bitcoins or the other cryptocurrencies after being enabled.

The following intrinsic idiosyncratic content threats of the currency are thus presented.

Risk for Business

The Loss of trust in digital currency: There is a strong degree of doubt over currencies' nascent existence. Speculators looking to gain from short-term or long-term ownership of digital currency have created a significant exchange activity on the online platforms. Cryptocurrencies aren't funded by the central bank, the national or the foreign entity, reserves, or other loans. The valuation of the cryptocurrencies is solely calculated by the value put on them by the market investors by their purchases, which implies that lack of faith will contribute to a breakdown of trading practices & an abrupt decrease in value.

3.1. The risk of Cyber Fraud

Since the cryptocurrency is effectively a cash currency, a significant number of criminals have been attracted; these criminals can hack into crypto exchanges and drain crypto-wallets & then compromise individual computers with the aid of cryptocurrency-stealing malware. As purchases are carried out on the internet, by means like spoofing/phishing & ransomware, hackers attack people, the service handling & the storage areas. To secure the purchased cryptocurrencies from fraud, investors must rely on the strength of their computer security systems and the security systems supported by third parties.

Besides, cryptocurrency is heavily dependent on unregulated businesses, including those that might lack adequate internal controls & may be more vulnerable than the controlled financial entities to fraud & robbery. Besides, the program has to be modified periodically & could be suspicious at times. The sourcing to providers of blockchain technologies will result in substantial risk disclosure by third parties.

Suppose keys are taken from a user's pocket. In that case, the attacker may completely impersonate the actual account owner & have the same access to money in the wallet as the original owner does. There's little in the way of recovery. When Bitcoins are exchanged out of account & the exchange is committed to blocking chain, the initial owner will permanently forfeit those assets.

3.2. The Operational risk

The power to revert a money exchange in a structured fashion falls from a centralized clearinghouse ensuring the transaction's legitimacy; still, no ability is available with the cryptocurrency. Furthermore, this absence of permeability is seen when the Bitcoin accounts become cryptographically encrypted. Access to money found in the account will almost surely not be recovered whether the "keys" to the account are misplaced or stolen

& therefore removed from the owner.

3.3. The risk of Regulation and compliance

Any countries that prohibit currency usage may state that transactions violate anti-money laundering legislation considering the global consequences. A single AML solution would not occur because of the difficulty and decentralized existence of Bitcoin & the large number of people involved: such as senders, the receivers (possibly tax avoiders), the processors (mining & trading platforms), and the currency exchanges.

3.4. Market risks

As currency traders are only on a demand basis, the market uncertainties are idiosyncratic. There is indeed a finite number of the currency, which ensures that supply considerations may be influenced & limited ownership may render it vulnerable to market manipulation. Besides, the currency can look more unpredictable than the other physical currencies and are fueled by the speculative demand & aggravated by the hoarding, provided its restricted adoption & lack of alternatives.

Therefore, providing the organization with an intrinsic material risk.

Many of the currency's intrinsic dangers often manifest & impact the organization by creating an external danger layer.

Further risks will include the expenses associated with mitigation concerning compliance with legal risk. Anti-money laundering & privacy legislation will have to be dealt with, including a myriad of the balances & restrictions, at the specific company level and the global level. In comparison, institutions would find themselves tasked with their very own schedule from separate jurisdictional law enforcement authorities, unable to conform to several different local & state laws.

To become all-inclusive in payment transmissions, the market challenge is strong as firms would need to accommodate & extend their offering, requiring a major revision of everything ready past due structures & networks. Besides, these upgrades to systems will still need to be constantly held up to date & consistent with the corporation's distribution structure & that of various third-party suppliers.

The tax danger is substantial as US individuals can attempt to bypass tax regulations, including the submission of FBAR (Report of International Bank & Financial Accounts) by anomalously storing money abroad. The Institutions which unwittingly or unintentionally endorse such circumvention may find themselves liable to penalties & fines. The exchange or transfer of currency and the documentation of these orders may also give rise to more company liabilities.

Cryptocurrencies are here to linger as technology progresses. Social approval and trust will take a little time, but both for the currency & the business, risks will stay the same, some seeming to become more material & elevated than before. Owing to the procedures involved, the crypto-currency industry may be overwhelming for rookies and experienced traders alike. To help you properly grasp the crypto-currency industry and how to exchange it, we have narrowed it down into six basic steps which are discussed in the next chapter.

Chapter 4: The Cryptocurrency trading steps

Owing to the procedures involved, the crypto-currency industry may be overwhelming for rookies and experienced traders alike. To help you properly grasp the crypto-currency industry and how to exchange it, we have narrowed it down into six basic steps:

1. Decide if you want to exchange cryptocurrencies.

2. Find out how the demand for cryptocurrencies functions.

3. Opening an Account

4. Build the trading strategy.

5. Pick the forum for cryptocurrency trading.

6. Open & track the first location, & close it.

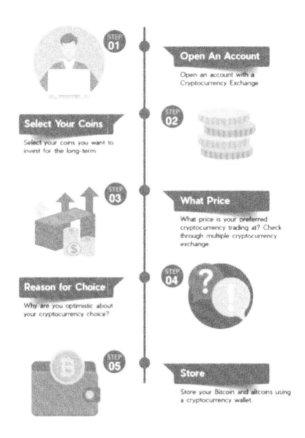

4.1. Decide if you want to exchange cryptocurrencies.

There are two routes to trading cryptocurrencies: (i) price speculation using the CFDs or (ii) purchasing digital currencies, hoping that their value will increase.

4.1.1. Trading the cryptocurrencies using CFDs

The CFD is the contract under which you choose to swap the difference in the cryptocurrency's price from the first moment you open the place to close it. Instead of taking control of cryptocurrency, you speculate about the stock interest. You would gain a profit when you open the long position & the cryptocurrency rises in value, so if it decreases in price, you will have a loss. The reverse is valid with a short position.

4.1.2. Cryptocurrency buying through an exchange.

Alternatively, to keep it in the digital wallet then profiting if it rises in value, you might opt to purchase a cryptocurrency, which implies that you take control of a part of digital currency directly.

You'd need to create a cryptocurrency wallet & an account with the cryptocurrency exchange until you can launch. This procedure will take several steps, & you may have to enter the waiting list for the account.

Before you start investing, the cryptocurrency industry functions distinctly other stock markets, which significantly contributes to study how it works & appreciate the language used to explain it.

4.2. How does it work?

The cryptocurrency market has become a decentralized virtual currency network, which indicates that it runs independently of a central server via peer-to-peer transaction testing. The transactions are applied to the blockchain, a shared database ledger that stores details through 'mining' when the cryptocurrencies are acquired & sold.

Cryptocurrencies are often popularly volatile, making it necessary to consider when the sector is going to move, from the ICOs & blockchain forks to the breaking news and government regulation.

4.3 How to Open an account

If you sell cryptocurrencies, you will open a spot even quicker instead of purchasing them. You wouldn't need a digital wallet or perhaps an exchange account. In reality, any account with such a leveraged trading supplier is all you need to trade through CFDs.

For IG, you will set up an account within minutes, and once you wish to put a trade, there is no requirement to add funds.

4.4 How to Create an account

For any trader, making a trading strategy is key to success, but much more so for the cryptocurrency traders since this sector will experience high volatility levels. It's a double-edged sword: the market is incredibly lucrative but risky to sell because of uncertainty. That's why risk assessment tools should be included in the trading plan, an overview of the

targets, which cryptocurrency that you intend to sell, and a trade entry & exit approach, defined as the trading strategy.

The way you evaluate the crypto-currency sector should also be included in the plan: either through the technical or the fundamental analysis. The Technical analysis concentrates on the market action of the cryptocurrency & its past trends. Simultaneously, the external factors & the macroeconomic evidence that influence the digital asset are analyzed in the fundamental analysis. It's indeed important to stay up to date on any news that might influence the market, whichever method you prefer, as cryptocurrencies are highly vulnerable to market sentiment.

4.5. Choose the cryptocurrency trading platform.

The trading platforms can help in smarter & faster ways to cryptocurrencies CFDs trade – with the personalized alerts, the interactive charts & the built-in risk management tools. It is indeed recommended that you trade through the IG trading platform by using:

- Web browser

- Your mobile apps

- Or the advanced 3rd-party platforms like mt4

4.6. Start by Opening, monitoring, and closing your 1st position.

Because there's no need to have a digital wallet when you can instantly initiate trading cryptocurrencies after opening the account with the IG & selected your platform.

All you have to do is to open the deal ticket for the preferred market; if you have agreed to sell ripple, ether, bitcoin, Litecoin, or some other cryptocurrency, & you'll find both a buying & a selling price mentioned. You may determine the size of the place & then opt to purchase in opening the long position or selling to enter a short position. Know, if it reaches a certain amount, you can introduce stops or restrictions to close the trade & secure the trade from unwanted risks.

In the 'available positions' segment of the dealing forum, you will track the position's benefit/loss. You only need to put an equal exchange in the opposite direction once you have determined that it is indeed time to close the spot.

4.7. The examples of Cryptocurrency trading

We have compiled two explanations of crypto-currency trades & their potential consequences to allow you to learn how to exchange cryptocurrencies.

E.g., CFD trading: ether selling.

You assume that the ether's price would decline in volume, a token of Ethereum network, & plan to fall short through selling ether over the US dollar (i.e., ether/USD).

You plan to offer five contracts (each equal to one ETH) to create a spot at this amount. The existing market price is around 200.

When the prediction is correct, if you had been correct, & the value of ether dropped against the U.S. dollar, it will help the exchange. Let's assume that the current market price is about 150. By purchasing five contacts to close the place at the selling price of 155, which would be marginally higher than the price because of spread, you will close the position & take the benefit.

Since the price has shifted 45 points in the favor, it will measure the trade's benefit as follows: 45 x 5 = 225$.

When your estimate is wrong

Even so, if the value of ether increased against the US dollar, it will close your place at a loss. Let's assume that aftermarket grew by fifteen points to 215, and you plan to leave the trade-so buy back five agreements at the selling price of 217. It will suggest that the loss was 17 x 5 = $85 for the place.

Chapter 5: 9 projects that could explode in 2021

Project 1: Ethereum

Ethereum is the technology that is the home to digital money, global payments, and apps. The community has created a booming digital economy, bold new ways for the creators to make online profits, and much more. It is open to all, and wherever you are in-country, what you need is the Internet.

The Ethereum aims to provide an **alternate protocol** for building decentralized applications, providing a different set of the trade-offs that we believe would be quite useful for the large class of decentralized applications, with the particular emphasis on the situations where the rapid development time, the security for small and seldom-used applications and ability of various applications to be quite effective. Ethereum achieves this by constructing the ultimate abstract foundation layer: the block-chain with an integrated Turing-complete computer language, enabling everyone to write the smart contracts and decentralized apps where they can generate their arbitrary rules for possession, transaction formats, and the state transition purposes. Name coin's bare-bone implementation may be written in the two code lines, and the other protocols such as currencies and the reputation systems may be developed in less than twenty. Smart contracts, the cryptographic "boxes" which contain value and only open it if those requirements are fulfilled, may even be created on top of the network, with much more control than that provided by the Bitcoin scripting because of additional powers of the Turing-completeness, valuation, the blockchain-awareness and the state.

VeChain Project 2(VET):

Vechain is a popular block-chain that extracts its value from those activities created by the ecosystem users to solve the real global economic problems. **VeChain** claims that blockchain technology is one of the new digital technology wave pillars, alongside emerging technologies like AR, VR, an AI, a IoT, 5G, and much more.

With the permanent and tamper-proof characteristics of technology, the block-chain, like an infrastructural technology, is ideal for unparalleled value and data sharing.

Which is in between a broad range of users in a trustless manner, improving the reliability and the validity of the knowledge transfer itself.

VeChain's goal of lowering the barrier and empowering existing block-chain technology companies to build demand and address real-world economic challenges has been obvious to us since the very beginning.

We also described the three main phases of block-chain growth – the Technological Consensus, the Market and Governance Consensus - then completely leverage technology that allows widespread public acceptance. These phases will be the foundation and strategy to allow VeChainThor block-chain to be embraced as the world's leading block-chain option.

Project 3: Stellar(XML):

Stellar is an accessible network to store and move money. Stellar allows it to develop, send, and digital exchange versions of all money types: the dollars, pesos, bitcoin, almost everything. It is structured such that all economic systems around the world will operate together on a common network. Stellar's Platform and the SDKs are willing to help you change the financial landscape, and the network's money connections will give only a small business the strength and scope of a multinational bank. And here is what you can do with the few code lines: **That Stellar**

Agreement Protocol, the framework for FBA. As with other Byzantine agreement protocols, the SCP does not allow any claims regarding attackers' logical actions. Unlike previous Byzantine agreement structures, which presuppose the unanimously agreed membership list, the SCP enjoys an inclusive membership that facilitates the organic network development. And Compared to decentralized proof work and the proof-of-stake structures, SCP has modest hardware and financial criteria, lowering the entry barriers and eventually opening up financial networks to new players.

Project 4: Uniswap (UNI)
UNI, the token of Uniswap Protocol, is live!

UNI contract address:

0x1f9840a85aF5bf1D1762F925BDADdC4201F984

60 percent of the UNI regeneration supply is reserved for Uniswap group holders, one-fifth of which (15 percent of the overall supply) has already been provided to former consumers.

For starters, UNI is accessible via 4 liquidity miners:

Development guided by the Society

After its conception, the Uniswap Protocol also acted as the trustless and extremely decentralized financial system.

Inspired by Ethereum's observation, we have long been dedicated to the values of unauthorized entry, security, and immutability, both indispensable components for the future where everyone in the world will approach financial services without the fear of prejudice or counterparty danger.

Now dealing with centralized day-to-day incumbents, Uniswap's performance to date – attained without the participation of the core evolution team following its deployment – suggests that there is a significant command for unauthorized financial services.

The agreement has in less than two years:

Supported over the $20 billion in value ($270k of which would be socks!) marketed across 250,000 and unique addresses across 8,484 different advantages.

Secured over $1 billion liquidity invested by 49,000 separate liquidity providers (LPs), obtaining $56 million in operation fees.

Emerged as the foundational Defi infrastructure, with combinations through hundreds of interfaces and apps.

Having proved to be fit for the highly decentralized financial infrastructure with the network that has flourished independently, Uni-swap is especially well placed for community-led growth, production, and self-sustainability. The UNI (ERC-20) adoption serves the function, facilitating mutual group ownership and the thriving, dynamic, and committed governance structure that will effectively lead the Protocol in the future.

Uni-swap has often adopted the principles of impartiality and minimization of trust: and government must be limited to where it should purely require. With this in view, the Uni-swap governance process is restricted to contributing to both the production and use of protocols and developing the wider Uni-swap environment.

In performing so, UNI formally enshrines Uni-swap as the public and self-sustaining infrastructure while continuing to preserve its indestructible and autonomous qualities closely.

Synthetix Project 5(SNX):

Synthetix is the cornerstone for derivatives trading in Defi, enabling anybody, everywhere, to achieve on-chain uncovering to the wide variety of securities.

Synthetix is the decentralized framework for the **generation** of synthetic assets based on Ethereum. These synthetic assets are also secured by Synthetix Network Token (SNX) that, when secured in the contract, allows synthetic assets to be issued (Synths). Such a pooled collateral model allows users to convert between Synths rightly to the smart contract without the counterparties' need. This process resolves the liquidity and the slippage problems faced by DEX. Synthetix promotes synthesized monetary currencies, cryptocurrencies (short or long), or products. SNX holders are encouraged to take their vouchers as they pay a pro-rated portion of the fees provided by the Synthetix operation. Exchange, based on offering to the network. It is also the privilege to take part in the web and receive fees provided by synth interchanges from which the values of the SNX voucher are obtained. Synthetix trading. The exchange shall not permit the dealer to possess SNX.

Project 6 Polkadot (DOT)

Polkadot's architecture is on track to provide the most scalable framework for certainty, scalability, and creativity.

Polkadot allows cross-blockchain transactions of some data or the asset, not just coupons. Connecting to Polkadot allows you to interact with a large range of blockchain technology on the Polkadot web. Polkadot offers unparalleled economic scalability by allowing a shared collection of validators to protect several block-chains. Polkadot offers transaction scalability by increasing transactions through several parallel block-chains. Use **Substrate** Platform to create a personalized block-chain in minutes. Attach your chain to the Polkadot and get the interoperability and protection right from day one. This simplicity of production lets Polkadot expand its network.

Project 7 AdaCardano (ADA)

Cardano is the block-chain forum for changemakers, the innovators, and the visionaries, with the resources and technology needed to build opportunities for many and few and bringing about sustainable international change.

Cardano is the proof-of-stake block-chain platform: and the first is to focus on peer-reviewed analysis and be built using evidence-based approaches. It integrates trailblazing technology to deliver unparalleled stability to decentralized devices, networks, and communities.

With the leading team of developers, Cardano exists to redistribute control from unaccountable systems to the periphery – to people – and to act as a catalyst for positive reform and development.

Cardano is a decentralized 3rd generation block-chain confirmation network and precursor to adding a cryptocurrency. It is the 1st block-chain network to emerge out from a theoretical philosophy to a research-driven methodology.

The Cardano framework was built completely and thoroughly and tested by a company-leading amalgamation of top developers and research specialists in blockchain and cryptography. It focuses strongly on sustainability, scalability, and clarity. It is a completely open-source platform that seeks to provide an internationally inclusive, equitable, and resilient platform for financial and social apps. One of the key objectives is to provide safe, stable financial services to someone who does not already have access to them.

Cardano was developed with protection among its initiating values. It's written in Haskell, a functional computer language. In the functional language such as Haskell, designing the framework utilizing pure functions is promoted, contributing to a layout where components are easily tested in isolation. Also, Haskell's advanced features allow us to employ a wide variety of powerful methods to ensure the correctness of code, such as implementing structured and functional requirements, comprehensive property-based checking, and running the simulation tests.

Project 8 Chainlink (LINK)

Chainlink's decentralized oracle network offers secure, tamper-proof inputs or the outputs for complex smart agreements in every block-chain.

The on-chain modules that ChainLink uses for agreements to acquire the external connectivity and the web node applications. We present both the straightforward on-chain agreement data aggregation method and the more well-organized off-chain consensus process. We also explain Chain Link's support for credibility and **protection** monitoring services, which allow consumers to make providers' educated choices and achieve robust service even under actively adverse circumstances. Finally, we describe an ideal oracle's attributes as the counseled for our security policy and set out potential future enhancements, like richly featured oracle scripting, data-source architecture updates, and confidential smart agreement execution.

Project 9 Fichain

Keep cryptocurrencies and then put them to work at the same time. **The cake** is the 1st truly open portal that delivers a consistent flow of cash for you.

DeFiChain, the dedicated cryptocurrency dedicated exclusively to decentralized finance (Defi) www.DeFichain.com.

By dedicating a blockchain's capabilities directly to decentralized finance, DeFiChain offers fast transaction throughput, reduced error risk, and smart features specifically built to achieve Satoshi's original goal: Build a stable alternate source of financial services constructed on the top of Bitcoin.

Bitcoin, defined in the original Satoshi whitepaper, is structured as digital currency, the store, and the value exchange. Evolution to the Ethereum and smart contracts have enabled enormous new features to be installed on a block-chain, but this progress has come with a cost. The idea of a single global operating system for all has created a structure that needs a dynamic codebase for contracts, poor throughput, and system governance difficulties.

DeFiChain focuses on decentralized finance as a relevant and important part of the block-chain group. Defi is said to be a dedicated block-chain that is uniquely designed for Defi implementations. DeFiChain is purposefully non-Turing-Complete, which may not endorse some functions other than those required for specifically be used in Decentralized Finance, which results in a block-chain that offers higher throughput and improved features exclusively for finance-related Apps. The benefit of a non-Turing full command is set such that there is a far lower risk for coding errors which have troubled Ethereum smart contracts earlier, such as DAO hacks or the famous Parity locked assets. While we must have certain smart contract languages like Turing is complete, it is reasonable to limit language capacities in favor of a more stable framework with substantially reduced attack vectors in the finance world.

Chapter 6: Understanding Cryptocurrency Exchange Rates

It comes as little surprise that most media twist news relevant to this subject every day, with cryptocurrencies, constantly occupying the headlines throughout the realms of investment. But today, when the exchange rates are steadily increasing again, much of the latest developments have been very optimistic. One must recognize cryptocurrency exchange rates generally before discussing why this matters.

6.1. The Cryptocurrency Exchange Rates

As for any commodity in which anyone may invest, the variable exchange rate determines the current value of every altcoin. The exchange rate is just a little above

US$8,100 right now in the case of the most dominant digital currency, Bitcoin. In other terms, anyone would have to spend $8,100 cash (plus dealer costs, depending on the cryptocurrency platform they are using) if they wish to buy a whole coin of this crypto commodity. Of course, even individuals who do not choose to acquire whole assets are rather reliant on exchange rates. Why? And indeed, the average exchange rate added to the coin would be focused on their interest in any cryptocurrency component. Therefore, if an investor were to invest 1/3 of a single bitcoin, that will take little north of $2,700 for their current investment. So, the digital coins' values converted into USD, Dollars, or some other fiat currencies are called cryptocurrency exchange rates.

6.2. Variable market rates of Digital coins

6.2.1 Do Exchange Rates Matter?

The explanation why exchange rates become important in the economy is the same as why regular product costs are important. They encourage customers to know precisely how much it costs to purchase anything. Thus, the above exchange rate of Bitcoin would be beneficial for someone who is saving money to invest in cryptocurrency. Also, when choosing whether the asset can be offered, exchange rates play an incredibly significant position. Those that may have acquired an altcoin a very long time ago, for example, will find it now to be a perfect better to transfer it. Why? Since some of the strongest highs of the current year have surpassed the present exchange rates. The investors who sell their investments will, thus, realize substantial investment returns.

6.2.2. Current Market Rates Trends

There appears to be a general theme when looking at Bitcoin rate background that echoes unpredictability & major price shifts. E.g., at the end of 2017, assets almost reached $20,000-coin worth only to drop over around two-thirds of this value in a single year. Today, it is increasing again & the price as it was at the end of December 2018 had almost tripled. As such, one of the key takeaways for all those seeking to evaluate the pace of Bitcoin would be that the price is so unpredictable that perfect results may be borderline unlikely. That's why so many investors love trading cryptocurrencies, where even the immense future profits help the excitement of making a correct prediction.

6.2.3. Do Exchange Rates May Change in Near Future?

As reported, the current Bitcoin rate is on the increase once again. With the overwhelming bulk of the other cryptocurrencies, that's also valid. For example, Ether has risen by $44, Litecoin is again nearing its current-year record, & Bitcoin Cash manages to surpass its 2019 level. What does aggregate economy mean about this? Ok, it offers us a reasonably clear indication of the direction the funds are going in. Namely, there appears to be a bull-like market where stocks are continually increasing & values are constantly rising. But it is not even realistic to identify how long this pattern would persist, and it now appears to be a perfect opportunity to make any transactions.

6.2.4. Can we Gauge Change in the Rates?

Several techniques could allow us to forecast the course & time frame during which a given exchange rate shift would take effect, as per market analysts. These mainly depend on an in-depth reading of cryptocurrency-related exchange rate maps. The whole principle of investing, that is, is focused on repetition in the asset's past. Consequently, looking at the popularity of Bitcoin in 2017, one might be tempted to assume that, yet another tremendous valuation surge may be on the horizon. If it is valid, relative to how big it might end up doing it at the end of the year, the current cost of $ 8,100 per coin seems minuscule.

It is important to remember, however, that any exchange rate map has its flaws. Second, the three-dimensional element that takes care of other incidents that involve the business is omitted from these tables. E.g., one of all laws passed in the field of crypto assets would not be aware by looking at prior price adjustments. Similarly, historical market trends do not regularly represent the number of entrants and emerging developments affecting this business. Comprehensive analysis that incorporates knowledge from multiple fields is also the safest approach in the long term to prevent wasting revenue.

Chapter 7: The Cryptocurrency Exchange Software

The Cryptocurrency exchange platforms, because of their groundbreaking features, have gained a prominent reputation over the past few years. They enable traders to easily buy or sell digital coins electronically as one of the most widespread networks open to investors who own decentralized properties.

Although cryptocurrencies facilitate stable and quick transfers, their most obvious influence rests on digital coins' capacity to store value. This suggests that they are seen as monetary investment instruments where owners hope to make capital returns. Ok, only investing in crypto exchange is the only way to recognize those benefits. Hence, this market's success.

7.1. The Brief History of the Crypto coin Exchange Software

Bitcoin trading sites were among the first to be functional networks of this kind. Bitcoin was, after all, the predominant popular cryptocurrency that attained historic prices & set countless benchmarks. However, there were also unsuccessful efforts to host the digital currency platform previous to these innovations.

E.g., in 2004, Australian Securities & Investments Commission closed down three big suppliers in that field. Similarly, the closure of another trade site in 2006 was supported by US Secret Service. The record of related cases continues until several of the first BTC trading venues start functioning at the end of 2009.

7.2. The Contemporary Developments & Trends

Any crypto trading platform prioritizes safety due to never-ending risks that originate in online community and place investors' investments in danger. This is achieved by implementing stringent anonymity, verification, and safe transaction policies. In comparison, exchange sites with religiously timed alerts that are seldom missed are legendary. They also allow improvements to user interfaces to meet the latest state of technology and investor desires.

What problems should Software for Cryptocurrency Trading solve?

The exchange program solves several various challenges, and it mainly focuses on multi-asset dealing. In other terms, it helps investors to hold several cryptocurrencies on the very same network & effortlessly share in transactions. Unlike certain crypto wallets that specialize in unique coins, a simple option to provide yet another place for one's investments is to utilize an exchange network. Because if a consumer might want to use any of the Bitcoin on the original public offering to acquire one of the new altcoins, they will do so without caring regarding compatibility.

Moreover, having an exchange is also favored with the available services. This involves current events, business graph-based portrayals, trained analysts that can be employed to counsel clients, and many more. Thus, comparatively, new buyers should take advantage of good affordable exchanges to maximize their lengthy benefit chances to the full.

Regardless of the reasons listed above, most investors will claim that exchanges become crucial when addressing an ancient problem that any market faces, which becomes crucial: higher broker fees. It is infamous for outrageous fees, forced to buyers' side of the market curve to acquire stocks & bonds. Nevertheless, with the digital coins, brokers' position has also been totally eroded in the same way that the need for financial intermediaries has also been diminished by decentralization. Thus, as there are no third-party mediators, exchanges are the motivating factor behind the falling transaction costs.

7.3. The Cryptocurrency Wallet Software

The Cryptocurrency wallet software contains observable & code-based networks where individuals secure their private keys that instigate automated transactions. Such structures act as online networks which provide unprecedented protections with one's crypto assets, sometimes attacked by hackers.

With improved features involving high-level encryption, unmatched protection, two-factor authentication, & many more, it is simple to protect one's credible cryptocurrency with the top crypto wallet tech. It's important to select carefully when shopping for the crypto wallet & only focus on those providers who can display formidable track records.

7.3.1. Cryptocurrency Wallet Software History

Originally, digital wallets were invented to endorse Bitcoin. Bitcoin also remains the most lucrative cryptocurrency present day, the founder in the sector. A program that supports private key storage was also developed when Satoshi Nakamoto founded the network: enter the Bitcoin Core GUI.

The Bitcoin Core enabled funds to be sent by individuals, and it was incredibly flawed. Second, it made it possible to create errors relevant to typing someone's address or missing private keys. This, along with the reality that the demand quickly led to hundreds of many other cryptocurrencies, attributed to Bitcoin Core's success becoming short-lived.

The single-coin wallets have undergone an existential crisis with the emergence of Ethereum, Ripple, & other altcoins. They were thus unable to store numerous forms of digital currency, in addition to not able to provide remarkable protection. Hypothetically, you will have to purchase different Ripple or Ethereum wallets to invest in Ripple & Ethereum.

7.3.2. Concepts & Modernization underlying

Given the above vulnerabilities, the development of the multi-platform applications was initiated by cryptocurrency miners, developers, & consumers. In other words, eventually, they switched to the development of the wallet, which might support several altcoins while still having the protection required. Furthermore, the original wallet app developers slowly branched out into various groups.

You will find items like online exchanges, laptop applications, & even hardware devices holding private keys during that stage. Thus, with the emergence of a modern wallet software, investors' differing risk levels are tackled. Many who were prepared to subject themselves to further danger for improved functionality, for instance, might switch to online alternatives. Even then, you were far more inclined to place your trust in the hardware wallets if you were risk averse.

7.4. Problems & their Solutions

A most worrisome concern encountered in the past by cryptocurrency investors was their failure to focus on third-party vendors. This concern was brought on by persistent hacks & multi-million-dollar damages. Fortunately, it effectively ended cyberattacks by building network-enforced applications. In other terms, as networks like Bitcoin & Ethereum built their storage tools, an alternative was offered to the investors that minimized the chance of robbery.

For instance, the Ethereum wallets' common features were optimized to fit the main features of the blockchain node of Ethereum. For example, they helped users easily set up the free & open wallet while completely embracing the revolutionary smart-contract technology.

Likewise, by moving its emphasis to online exchanges, Bitcoin has modernized its strategy. That's also because there has been an unprecedented increase in the number of transactions conducted on this website. The network required the storage software where the online fund transactions were quickly generated to catch pace with ever-growing demand.

7.5. Exchange Platforms

Bit stamp:
Bit-stamp is the bitcoin exchange located in Luxembourg. It makes it easy to exchange fiat money, bitcoin, and other cryptocurrencies. Enables USD, EUR, GBP, Bitcoin, XRP, Ethereum, Litecoin, Bitcoin cash, XLM, Link, GMO Web, USD

Coin, or the PAX money transfers.

The business was established as the European-focused competitor to the dominant bitcoin exchange of Mt. Gox. Although the organization invests in US dollars, it accepts unlimited fiat money transfers only via the Single Euro Payments Area of the European Union, a system for exchanging money among European bank accounts.

Bit stamp provides an API to enable clients to view & manage the accounts using custom apps.

Binance:

Binance is the cryptocurrency exchange that offers a forum for the exchanging of different cryptocurrencies. Since about January 2018, Binance was the world's biggest cryptocurrency exchange in terms of trade value. Binance was developed by Changpeng Zhao, the developer who had previously produced high-frequency trading tools.

Bitfinex:

Bitfinex provides order books with the highest liquidity level, enabling customers to trade Bitcoin quickly, the Ethereum, EOS, Litecoin, the Ripple, NEO, and several other cryptocurrencies with zero slippage. Liquidity suppliers may earn returns by offering liquidity to traders who wish to deal with the leverage. Funding is marketed on the order book at varying prices and hours. Bitfinex facilitates up to the 10x leverage investing by supplying customers with an approach to peer-to-peer financing. Bitfinex provides the suite of order forms to provide traders the resources they need for each case. Please find out more from our most sophisticated forms of algorithmic instructions. Arrange your workspace to suit your needs: compose your interface, select between the themes, and set up alerts. The security of user accounts and funds is our top priority. Read more regarding our security capabilities and integration.

Chapter 8: How the Cryptocurrency Mining Works?

The Cryptocurrencies are digital currencies that operate independently of all banks & governments, but they can be exchanged or speculated on like the physical currency. Bitcoin was launched in the year 2009, and it was 1st decentralized cryptocurrency. After that, many more cryptocurrencies, referred to as altcoins, have been launched.

While bitcoin remains the market leader, other cryptocurrencies include bitcoin cash, bitcoin gold, Litecoin, ripple, ether, EOS, stellar (XLM) & NEO, which can be a challenge in the future due to rise in the demand, expansion in applications, & the technological advancement.

Manufacturers first issued/Crypto coins in small runs called the blocks, unlike the standard currency, which is printed, then certified, and placed into circulation by the mint. Only a small number of the blocks are in use at a certain given time & can be then harvested in the crypto miners' blockchains. This technology of the Blockchain acts as a thorough transaction background of all the currencies linked or chained) together. Such blocks define in sequential order all transactions through which a coin has been passed. The Cryptocurrency mining program is had used by miners to retrieve comprehensive transaction history from such blocks to guarantee the coin's validity.

The complexity of crypto mining arises from measuring how a coin's past can be transformed into the 256-bit coded numerical & letter string. Users may generate strings to be attached to the coin's blockchain through measuring strings & blocks. Per each megabyte of the code, they uncover and "mine," consumers are then charged.

Today, blockchain mining is seldom profitable for someone without a specialized mining rig due to exponential computing capacity & crypto-currency mining tools. To create collaborative mining pools, clients have begun taking to combining their resources, & many investors had also turned to the cryptocurrency exchanges to circumvent skyrocketing mining revenue & invest in the popular coins.

Mining is easy when the blockchain has a few people doing this, & people could even set up the "big iron" computers within their own homes to make extra income.

For those that like to make safe transfers without leaving a trace, this makes them appealing.

As this has become more commonplace, the overall valuation of crypto mining has declined & only those with large machines will remain successful. Conversely, many individuals who want to be involved but could not commit to the mining choose to invest in cryptocurrencies.

Unlike trading securities, going to invest in cryptocurrencies doesn't come with any such government oversight. If you'd like to give it a shot, you will be on your own.

8.1. How Safe Is Cryptocurrency?

Because some governmental supervision does not come with cryptocurrencies, missing coins become lost for sure. Human error is often a crypto-security threat; even losing your password will permanently lock the cryptocurrency away.

The Crypto users are vulnerable to assaults by malware & ransomware that keep the details hostage and when criminals grab coins from you, recognized as crypto heists. To use the victim's device & to mine the blockchains for themselves, crypto mining operations should defend themselves from crypto jacking assaults. Hackers may steal dedicated mining machines.

Antivirus security tools are way to defend from ransomware through crypto mining since they help restrict hackers' entry into the device. The inter authentication tools which secure the operation against internal attacks are often used in several crypto platforms.

As all currency advantages are automatically negated if they do not secure the investment, they should choose a platform that places a premium on protection.

8.2. The Bitcoin Currency Trading

The Bitcoin price, like standard currency and shares, is described by the ticker symbol. You'll generally see it identified as BTC, but it is mentioned as XBT by several cryptocurrency exchanges. Amongst many people, Bitcoin listings drew interest, which contributed to a rise of users across the globe who started crypto mining.

The bulk of crypto exchanges already take place on dedicated app platforms for the cryptocurrency exchange that enable you to swap coins for many other cryptocurrency types & less regularly for fiat cash. There are centralized & de-centralized exchanges, with the key distinction between the two being the "middle-man" traders' existence.

The Cryptocurrency wallet app saves coins for anyone, enabling you to purchase & sell crypto, much like standard exchanges, computers, or a real piece of the hardware. Crypto is often exchanged on markets where, not too unlike stock prices, coin prices fluctuate. People may exchange one crypto with another or, if allowed, for fiat currency.

Bitcoin is perhaps the most common among blockchain-based & tokenized currencies because it was first throughout the industry. The Bitcoin digital wallet is becoming a popular software that stores required details to execute BTC transactions. It is often used to keep Bitcoin tokens & store them. Some technologists have also built actual hardware that, much as standard currencies, BTC users will carry them to shops & use to invest their Bitcoins.

The Bitcoin wallet is becoming a popular piece of software that stores required details to execute BTC transactions.

Some consumers, though, have become unhappy with increasing Bitcoin prices and have switched to 'altcoins' then. These alternate cryptocurrencies, which then, in turn, affect their value, have become increasingly common. Altcoins are mentioned on a chart of cryptocurrencies that contains both currency forms and trade offers. Here is another list of more popular altcoins:

Ethereum: This open-source distributed altcoin supports the power to create smart contracts among groups of users. The Ethereum has been one of the most common altcoins now in operation, as it follows the same blockchain technologies like Bitcoin.

Dash: The Dash shares with Bitcoin quite enough code as Ethereum does, but its creators have differentiated it by heavily optimizing cryptographic hashes that control it.

Litecoin: Litecoin came along just as it was beginning to get pricey for crypto mine for the BTC tokens as being one of the early altcoins. Under the X11 license, the program that drives it was issued, so other currencies could easily be built on Litecoin.

Zcash: While both cryptocurrencies are privately developed, Zcash is built on the blockchain protocol incorporating hashes with the additional digits. This allows the reproduction of Zcash tokens more complicated.

The Bitcoin & the numerous altcoins both have upsides & pitfalls in today's economic environment & may provide distinct choices. No one cryptocurrency is the greatest. To help mitigate these disadvantages, those planning to invest typically create a crypto portfolio with varied coins.

The development of the crypto portfolio is not that far from the construction of a conventional investment portfolio. When one begins to lose value, adding several cryptocurrencies to the wallet will help you survive the storm—keeping an eye on exchanges. Until you invest in some new network or crypto coins, making sure to perform a comprehensive analysis. Most notably, don't ever let anyone convince you that the strongest overall is the cryptocurrency. They may have a personal interest in getting you to believe that!

Follow these rules, and these latest financial frontiers will be more than capable of braving you. Check out tools, like a comprehensive summary & buyer's guide, to know more about applications that embrace cryptocurrencies.

Be sure also to review TEC's Cloud-based Tech Professional Purchase Tips such that you are informed when obtaining licenses with the relevant questions & considerations.

8.3. Cryptocurrency Mining Software

It's no wonder that you have been fascinated by cryptocurrencies, both as the new medium for secure, private, & reliable transfers but rather as a way to unleash the power of computation to earn some cash. You would need to set up the necessary technology to mine such money if you are willing to create Bitcoin mining or the business owner looking to utilize your corporation's strong machines for mining. It isn't simple, nor is it meant to be.

The fact is, to tackle this idea, there are a multitude of methods, a whole range of cryptocurrencies to mine, as well as a ton of tech solutions. We will learn about the technologies you want & what we need out of the applications to mine cryptocurrencies more effectively. While becoming the most common & well-known cryptocurrency, we will also speak a little something about never pigeonholing the energies exclusively through Bitcoin.

There is no one correct approach to it that fits everybody, based on budget, bandwidth, & the amount of patience. It is somewhat demanding, & of course, quite pricey, computation to "rapidly" mine cryptocurrencies. With the right program, slower methods are feasible, mirrored, to yet get the job completed. That trick is to get the proper mining structure that encourages this cryptocurrency.

Crypto mining software aims to run parallel calculations on the data blocks that produce a currency unit when the threshold is issued after these algorithms are solved. A set of blocks are attached to this resolved info, thus blockchain money, which is cross-dependent & in some manner difficult to forcefully modify or vandalize. You will want the crypto mining programs to reach elevated hash rates to enable quicker, more simultaneous calculations, long story short.

There is several cryptocurrency mining software around here, several of which may mine several currency types, while others concentrate on one specific currency.

Chapter 9: Cryptocurrency investment tips

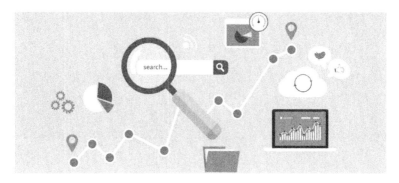

All right, all of you, I have the coaching cap on. Maybe I'll also get the bit worked up! There are many items users will need to remember before they say farewell to the dollars and welcome to Bitcoin or the Ether.

1. There are unpredictable cryptocurrencies. Extreme rises and downs go into the valuation of cryptocurrencies. Bitcoin's worth shifted between $800 and $30,000 in 2017! Somebody's sneezing and lowering the cost it is dangerous to trade in crypto currencies, to mention the minimum all investment brings an amount of risk, of course. But particularly when it falls to the hard-earned income, one can always prevent needless risks. Don't use the financial potential to play poker.

2. Dozens of unknowns are there. There is also a tonne that requires to be straightened out on how the cryptocurrencies function. Realize about that as well;

nobody else understands who Bitcoin's inventor is! Just a limited number of citizens around the country, generally speaking, grasp the mechanism and learn how to run it. Ignorance leaves. One insecure I still warn individuals that if they can't describe the finances to a 10-year-old, to begin with, they have no business engaging in them. You are lining yourselves up to perform a dumb thing.

3. For illegal operations, cryptocurrencies could be used. Cryptocurrencies can be used by individuals who wish to stay anonymous to circumvent bank or government controls to create shady transactions, mostly on the black marketplace. In the field of cryptography, currency laundering is still a concern. Now, listen to me on this: I'm not suggesting that anyone who utilizes cryptocurrencies is a poor individual. But I'm suggesting that the crypto environment is a perfect location for them if anyone tries to conduct illegal activities and escape being watched.

4. The Cryptocurrencies have a return probability that is unproven. The cryptocurrency exchange is like betting. Since private to the consumer is traded without any connection to regulatory requirements, there is no trend for its value to grow and fall. For development stock mutual funds, one cannot forecast improvements or measure

returns as one can. There's not enough evidence or adequate integrity to build a long-term cryptocurrency-based investment strategy.

5. Investments are still unpredictable, but according to User Surveys, some analysts claim that cryptocurrency is among the riskiest investment options out there. However, some of the top assets are still virtual currencies. CNBC projected relatively early this year that by completing 2018, the crypto-currency industry is anticipated to hit a size of $1 trillion. These guides will help you make intelligent decisions if users're looking to participate in cryptocurrencies.

6. Exchanges of Analysis: Before people spend one dollar, understand cryptocurrency transactions. These websites have the means to purchase and trade digital currency. However, as per Bitcoin.com, there are 500 markets to select from. Before going ahead, do the homework, read the reviews and speak with more seasoned investors.

7. Knowing how the digital currencies should be kept: You need to save them if you purchase cryptocurrencies in your wallet. Simultaneously, several various styles of wallets exist and have their advantages, technological specifications, and protection. Just like exchanges, before buying, you can study the storage options.

8. Expand the Investment opportunities

Diversifying is a cornerstone to every successful investing policy, and when you trade-in crypto currency, that still holds real. For starters, do not even place all of the money into Bitcoin only because it's the title you recognize. There are hundreds of choices, and it's better to distribute the investment through many currencies.

Plan for Fluctuation: The demand for crypto currencies is unpredictable, so be equipped for highs and lows. You'll encounter drastic market changes. If the financial fund or emotional health can't manage it, cryptocurrencies may not be a wise option for everyone. Right here, blockchain is all the hype, but mind, it's still in its development. Challenges come from engaging in anything different, so be ready. Do the homework and spend modestly to begin if users intend to join.

9.1. May I make investments in cryptocurrencies?

Here's the deal: Get an emergency budget that can finance three or six months of bills if people 're out in default, plus you're still spending 15 percent of the profits in growth equity mutual financial resources, which are dozens of times better than bitcoin, but users can decide to mess about with cryptocurrencies.

But I'd like to advise the reader to be ready to tell goodbye-o to the money when individuals invest in cryptography. This isn't a healthy way of creating money. Dozens of entrepreneurs who agree with us are here.

The new money structure is weak, as per Deutsche Bank. Deutsche Bank predicts virtual currencies will grow to almost 300 million consumers by 2030. Deutsche Bank indicates in the "Imagine 2030" study that, when appetite for privacy and a much more decentralized payment mode rises, virtual money might potentially overtake cash one day.

Ilias Louis Hatzis is the editor and weekly writer of Mercato Blockchain Company AG at DailyFintech.com

Typically, we begin to read market projections of Bitcoin increasing to a million flips a coin this year. I was not a huge fan of projections regarding rates. Some are doing them correctly, and others are getting them incorrect. Predictions for prices are for short-term rises, which are typically quite fickle.

But I did read a fascinating observation in the press a week ago. Deutsche Bank made a very brave comment. The

German Bank released a study report named Imagine 2030. In this research, the bank notes that cryptocurrencies are simply extensions to the existing money transfer scheme at present. They may be alternatives, though, in the coming decade.

Deutsche Bank estimates that the total of consumers of cryptocurrencies would rise 4x, hitting 300 million in the coming ten years. This creation is nearly similar to that of the Internet in the first 30 years.

9.2. Is Cryptocurrency the Destiny of Wealth?

There are stunning similarities between both the Web and cryptography. The Web was officially supported and mainly used in a scholarly context before Mosaic. Yet progressive politicians have agreed to legalize commercial Internet operations. Although the Internet's commercial usage began with several individuals and organizations not learning how to communicate or utilize the Internet, rails were placed in the position that would ultimately modify anything.

Not that far away are the break-out years of streamlined usage and tremendous user development. There is ample potential, wealth is here, and conditions such as economic empowerment and liberty are suitable.

Still, for all of this to occur, there has been one major x-factor that is unknown. How can cryptocurrency tackle authorities? We require enlightened politicians who will legitimize cryptocurrencies for Deutsche Bank's prophecy to come real. The study states:' First, in the view of authorities and regulators, they must appear legal.' Truly!

Control in Crypto may be right around the edge. Cryptocurrencies could become legal replacements for fiat currencies as regulatory barriers are resolved. Without a brutal war, many regimes would not sit by and surrender hold over the money flow. Undoubtedly, bitcoin and other safe coins will offer the pathway for universal acceptance, with better supervision by regulatory authorities.

A segment entitled "The demise of paper money?" is what's much more interesting about the research. It's somewhat crazy, given that this study arrives from an immense global fund. Banks are just beginning to understand what citizens in the crypto-currency world have understood for a time. That's great news, though!

Fiat might not be the true victim of encryption, but acrylic cards. We've started replacing our cash quietly for years now. Cash, debit, and credit cards are increasingly

becoming redundant, and as crypto adoption grows, they may proceed on this path. We also changed from physical money and tokens to internet transfers and transactions as you thought of evolution Credit/Debit Cards. Plastic cards are now obsolete because of the spike in smartphone payments by AliPay, WeChat Pay, and Paypal. Blockchain has several benefits over credit cards. However, the fundamental distinction among the two is that all purchases and transactions are performed with the customer's total permission. In Deutsche Bank's view, disposable cards could perish. If the popularity of cryptocurrencies grows, believing that credit cards would vanish is just reasonable. We would no longer require them.

Although, there are still complicated assumptions. The 20/20 is Hindsight. Everybody needs to accept this right away. We may taste a world that is democratic. Things are time-consuming, but the timer has started. Cryptocurrencies are much more common than you believe they have been. Almost 18 percent of customers located in the US either hold at least one virtual money or have possessed one in the old days, as per a study. Like any other else in existence, Crypto could be both positive and bad. The true meaning of cryptocurrencies is unknown among many citizens since they are just based on commodity investing guided by price and uncertainty.

Crypto has a special strategy that leaves fiat money redundant. Cryptocurrency encourages individuals to become their independent bank and means of payment. Regulatory and technological problems are the major ones. User-adoption is the determining element on which crypto replaces currency. Yet blockchain can render the future appear entirely different until it is mounted and incorporated into our lives, in respects we could only hope to grasp.

Chapter 10: Is Cryptocurrency the Future of Money?

10.1. A Cryptocurrency Era

In current years, cryptocurrencies have been a worldwide phenomenon, but more remains known regarding this emerging tech. The innovation and

Its potential to challenge existing financial processes has several questions and concerns revolving about it.

The Cryptocurrencies are digital currencies that operate independently of all banks & governments, but they can be exchanged or speculated on like the physical currency. Bitcoin was launched in the year 2009, and it was 1st decentralized cryptocurrency. After that, many more cryptocurrencies, referred to as altcoins, have been launched.

While bitcoin remains the market leader, other cryptocurrencies include bitcoin cash, bitcoin gold, Litecoin, ripple, ether, EOS, stellar (XLM) & NEO, which can be a challenge in the future due to rise in the demand, expansion in applications, & the technological advancement.

Recently, Stanford Law College instructor Joseph A. Grundfest sat down to explore how bitcoin is being utilized, where bugs have been created, and the coming years' promise for this innovation. As a retired Stock and Exchanges Commission Commissioner and a financial systems specialist, Scholar Grundfest is best qualified to speak on cryptocurrencies' prospects.

10.2. The reality regarding insecure structures

Bitcoin and some other cryptocurrency proponents contend that these financial networks are fundamentally untrustworthy structures - that is, they are not explicitly connected to any state, administration, or body. They will say that since it is not reliant on.

Grundfest states that it's not completely true, irrespective of whether they believe it's a positive or poor thing. Cryptocurrencies are not at all unsecure. They are also relying on the underlying cryptocurrencies fueling infrastructure such as Bitcoin, mostly based in China. By forcing its will on the data brokers who hold them going, the Chinese authority might potentially permit modifications to cryptocurrencies at such a basic stage. The relation of Facebook to cryptocurrencies, Libra, has been pumped in certain places to solve several financial problems. The framework was developed to promote foreign transfers and remove excessive charges for transactions.

The objective is commendable, Lecturer Grundfest admits, but he considers that the method is seriously flawed. He doesn't even see the implementation of yet another cryptocurrency as the correct way to decrease money transfers and that he does not completely comply with the efforts by Facebook to bypass conventional financial structures.

Conversely, Prof Grundfest contends that it would've been a good strategy for Facebook to generate its very own bank, which might act as its users' main financial organization. The business could have concentrated on creating banking structures tailored to each country or area, discussing regulatory requirements, and driving down expenses. If these were developed and people's confidence was developed, it would make sense actually to attach one by one and build a worldwide system.

10.3. Is the secure coin a solution?

Secure coins have risen in importance to reverse cryptocurrency with true value resources, more or less the same way the U.S. currency was used to be on a gold level of quality. Many currencies or commodity markets could be those assets, practically any of them.

With this method, there are a lot of difficulties Grundfest gets. In turn, for one, it reconstructs a structure that already works. The other issue would be that since it is not convenient to audit and supervise as conventional currencies, it would make it possible for customers to commit fraud. The webinar highlighting several of the better cryptocurrency apps was closed by Prof Grundfest. People who live in weak-currency nations, for example, could be safer off trading in Bitcoin than purchasing local bonds and stocks.

The current prospects of Cryptocurrency are still quite much in the query. Supporters see unlimited power, while opponents see very little risk. Prof Grundfest stays a skeptic, but he does agree that there are many apps where a feasible alternative is cryptocurrencies.

The cryptocurrency is a virtual currency produced and

regulated by sophisticated encryption methods such as cryptography. With the emergence of Bitcoin in 2009, Cryptocurrencies enabled the transition from becoming an academic idea to (digital) reality.1 Although Bitcoin gained a rising audience in successive times in April 2012, it grabbed substantial investor and press interest as it exploded at a historic $267 per bitcoin since soaring 11-fold in the previous two months. At its peak, Bitcoin featured a market price of over $3 billion. Still, briefly after that, a 50 percent drop triggered a fierce discussion about the coming years of cryptocurrencies in particular and Bitcoin in particular. Can these alternate solution currencies ultimately supersede traditional currencies and become as widespread again someday as various currencies? Are indeed cryptocurrencies a fleeting trend that will fade out for a considerable time to come? For Bitcoin, the problems lie.

As organizational money comes on the market, some financial analysts' experts expect a big transition in crypto is coming. The chance that crypto would be sailed mostly on Nasdaq would further increase access to the blockchain, and it utilizes as just a substitute to traditional currencies.4 A few assume that an authenticated exchange exchanged fund (ETF) is all that crypto requires. An ETF would defy.

Bitcoin is the centrally controlled currency that utilizes peer-to-peer innovation, allowing the system to collectively perform all operations such as currency approval, transaction handling, and verification.6 While this decentralization makes Bitcoin available of government deception or intervention, and the opposite is that there seems to be no core authority to make sure that things go smoothly or to make sure that things go smoothly. Via a "mining" method that involves efficient machines to resolve complex equations and smash numbers, Bitcoins are generated virtually. They were currently generated every 10 minutes at the pace of 25 Bitcoins and would be restricted at 22 million, a number estimated to be surpassed in 2140,77.

These aspects render Bitcoin radically distinct from a conventional currency, which would be supported by the gov't's full trust and credit. Fiat currency distribution is a closely centralized operation managed by the central bank of a country. Hypothetically, although the bank controls the sum of currency distributed in compliance with all its financial policy goals, there is no maximum bound on the sum of the issuance of those currencies. Furthermore, regional currency reserves are normally insured by the government entity toward banking crises. But on the other side, Bitcoin doesn't have any such support systems. The worth of a Bitcoin relies solely on what consumers can pay when in time for it. Often, consumers with Bitcoin accounts have no way to get it back if a Bitcoin company packs up.

10.4. The Bitcoin Future Prospective

The long-term outlook for bitcoin seems to be the topic of a lot of discussions.   While well-known crypto evangelists evolve in the financial press, Harvard University Instructor of Economics and the Public Policy Kenneth Rogoff indicates that perhaps the "overwhelming impression" between crypto advocates becomes that over the coming five years, the maximum "market capitalization of the cryptocurrencies could boom, growing to $6-10 [trillion].

The investment class's historic instability is "no excuse to panic" he adds. He, however, expressed his confidence as well as that of Bitcoin's "crypto evangelist" vision as virtual gold, finding it "crazy," saying that this long-term worth is "more probable to be $120 than $120,000."

Rogoff argues that Bitcoin's use is limited to transactions, unlike physical gold, making it more vulnerable to a bubble-like collapse. Besides, the cryptocurrency's energy-intensive verification process is "vastly less efficient" than systems that rely on "a trusted central authority like a central bank."8.

10.5. Elevating investigation

The main advantages of Bitcoin's decentralization and money transfer confidentiality have also crafted it a preferred commodity for a server of criminal activities, which include laundering money, drug trafficking attempting to smuggle, and supplying weapons. This has drawn prominent governmental and regulatory bodies, such as a Financial Crimes Investigation Network (FinCEN), an SEC, and the FBI and National Security Agency (DHS).FinCEN authorized regulations in March 2014 that described digital currency transactions and the administrators as the cash service companies, helping to bring them inside the govt regulation scope.9 In May of the same year, the DHS shuddered an account retained at Wells Fargo for Mt. Gox, the biggest Bitcoin market accusing that it violated anti-money laundering rules.10 11 And in October, the New York Dept of Finance

10.6. Bitcoin alternative solutions

Bitcoin's popularity and prominence since its introduction, amid its recent problems, has culminated in a variety of businesses introducing alternate cryptocurrencies, including such:

Litecoin-Litecoin is currently recognized as the greatest rival of Bitcoin and is intended more quickly to process relatively small transactions. As per founder Charles Lee, it was established in October 2011 as "a coin which is silver to the gold of Bitcoin."13 Unlike most of the massive desktop horsepower needed for Bitcoin mining, the Litecoin could be mined by a standard desktop pc. The optimum threshold of Litecoin is 85 million, five times the 22 million thresholds of Bitcoin. It has a payment processing period of about 3.5 minutes, around one-fourth that of Bitcoin.

Ripple – The Ripple has been decided to launch by OpenCoin, a business established by new tech innovator Chris Larsen in 2013. The Ripple, or Bitcoin, is indeed a money system and payment method. The XRP, which has a logical basis as Bitcoin, seems to be the currency part. In addition to Bitcoin transfers, which can require as much as ten minutes to validate, the payment system makes the transferring of money of any commodity to another individual on a Ripple platform within minutes.

MintChip- the MintChip is, in reality, the development of a government entity, actually a Royal Canadian Vault, unlike most other cryptocurrencies. MintChip is indeed a prepaid card that carries and can safely exchange digital value through one device to another. Like Bitcoin, MintChip does not require identity information; it's often funded by a real currency, a Canadian dollar, except for Bitcoin.

10.7. What happens In the Coming years?

Any of the challenges which cryptocurrencies face, such as the fact that a machine crash would delete one's digital wealth or that a hacker may ransack a digital bank, may be solved in the future through technological developments. What would be more challenging to solve is the underlying phenomenon that cripples cryptocurrencies. The more successful they get, the more legislative and political attention they will expect to draw, eroding their creation's basic principle.

While the number of merchants embracing cryptocurrencies has risen slowly, they remain clearly in the small group. They must first achieve general recognition among users of cryptocurrencies to being even more widely used. Nevertheless, except for the electronically adept, their relative difficulty compared to the traditional currencies would discourage most individuals.

The cryptocurrency that intends to be part of the conventional financial structure will have to follow wildly differing specifications. It will have to be numerically abstract (to deter theft and hacker assaults) but simple to comprehend for customers; centrally controlled but with sufficient security and security for customers; and maintain consumer privacy without becoming a platform for tax avoidance, money smuggling as well as other illegal practices. Is it conceivable that the most common cryptocurrency in the next few years will also have characteristics that fell between highly controlled paper money and today's cryptocurrencies because these are enormous requirements to meet? If the probability seems distant, there is no question that perhaps the performance (or absence thereof) of Bitcoin in grappling with the difficulties it poses as the main cryptocurrency at present will decide the fate of many other cryptocurrencies throughout the coming years.

10.8. Will You Spend on Cryptocurrencies?

It might be wise to handle your 'expenditure' in the same manner you would approach some other highly risky company if you are contemplating engaging in cryptocurrencies. In many other terms, realize that you take the danger of destroying the bulk, if not many, of the investment. As mentioned before, aside from what a consumer can pay for it at the moment in time, a cryptocurrency seems to have no inherent worth. This renders it very vulnerable to massive market volatility, which then raises an investor's chance of failure.

For, e.g., on April 12, 2014, Bitcoin plummeted from $250 to around $140 within seven hours. 18 If you could not handle that sort of uncertainty, search around for more tailored assets to you.

Though opinions on the value of Bitcoin as the asset appear to be strong, divided supporters refer to the small supply and rising use as valuation generators. At the same time, critics see it as another massive bubble claim that a cautious investor will do well to escape.

A discussion over the future and those of several cryptocurrencies have ignited the rise of Bitcoin. Its popularity since its 2008 introduction has motivated the development of substitute cryptocurrencies like the Ethereum, Litecoin, and the Ripple, notwithstanding Bitcoin's recent problems. There will be very widely different parameters for a cryptocurrency that intends to be a piece of the conventional financial structure.

If the prospect seems distant, there is little question that the ability or inability of Bitcoin to cope with the difficulties it confronts in the coming years could decide the fate of several other cryptocurrencies.

Chapter 11: Crypto Asset Management

After the UK-based Robo-advisor and the online income manager, Nutmeg exceeded GBP 2 billion in assets under planning last year, the next transformation process has been meeting substantial milestones. However, for cryptocurrencies, the latter degree of centralized implementation and recommendations is less the scenario, which faces various difficulties that create it unattractive to less knowledgeable shareholders.

Crypto investment management instruments are rapidly emerging with the straightforward need to support retail stockholders with their business investigation. The incentive is evident for the corporations behind such platforms: the business market value of cryptocurrencies is approximately $500 billion, and markings of stabilization are beginning to show.

A much more thoughtful market also implies that the less informed investors are probable to stick their noses in, needing a forum that provides simpler access than the disintegration that presently defines the exchange ecosystem in tandem.

11.1. Streamlined crypto management's appeal.

It is still more difficult to buy cryptocurrencies than to purchase regular equity. As cryptocurrencies tempt new customers, more market players have become conscious of the demand for simple tools engineered for investors of all skill levels to handle crypto portfolios.

Currently, fresh traders should first locate a wallet that acknowledges a cryptocurrency they want to exchange, then discover an exchange before finishing a multidimensional and long verification process that identifies their preferred coin. They should spread out over wallets and transfers once they have entered the market if they want to broaden their assets. While it's feasible, the process's complexity stays a major obstacle to the entrance for several would-be investors. The issue is recognized by most in the market. The Blox CEO Alon Murdoch suggests that keeping a record and maintaining your crypto resources is not a walk in the playground, even for more professional ones, or particularly for them." It might be a challenge to understand where the coins are held, how they execute and their real-time profile.

Consequently, a method that is now popular in a more conventional money system, asset planning, is being introduced by some businesses. Crypto wealth management systems streamline the process rather than having to maintain numerous accounts and wallets by assisting users in strengthening their varied holdings while offering enhanced portfolio strategic tools at the same time.

There have already been many funds that give the management of crypto assets and spend on behalf of the clients. This method has shown outstanding growth so far, with one corporation, the Bitwise Asset Management, revealing a 52 percent return after perceiving crypto-specific finance in fewer than five months. With the investment class's increasing popularity, systemic investors have chosen to take notification with research indicating that in 2017 the number of crypto investments might double.

Nevertheless, most investors still handle their assets in an ecosystem. Many other operating systems have developed themself as go-to instruments, with current models arising every day.

11.2. Figuring Via an Emerging Market

Various markets have arisen in the crypto business, selling a mix of cryptocurrencies but not a complete list. Since several platforms are not compliant with all the wallets, this presents a problem for buyers, contributing to problems when handling a diverse variety of funds.

Crypto wealth management systems aim to automate the mechanism without resorting to the third entity or advisor to handle the assets of participants to address the dilemma. These methods provide a smoother road to entry and growth for ordinary investors who lack broad and comprehensive knowledge of the field.

Many tools aim to optimize crypto traders' wealth processing, and several have already proven their effectiveness. The Murdoch's Blox, for instance, provides consumers a convenient way to consolidate their various wallets and share accounts in a singular spot.

The corporation's software enables users to simultaneously control several portfolios and facilitate automated integration such that trades and transactions by clients can all be automatically modified. In comparison, through blockchain, the platform promotes wider usage. Traders may utilize CDT tokens to activate premium services and, by utilizing the firm's portfolio management software, can gain coins.

Like Iconomi, others offer more conventional wealth management resources that enable traders to build their specific asset classes and mixes to meet their risk appetite. The Other blockchain-based network, Blackmoon, operates a cryptocurrency platform that helped orchestrate software for wealth holders to monitor consumer portfolios and to monitor their assets from institutional traders. A much more democratic strategy has also been established by some firms, encouraging traders to participate in other investors' funds and plans, such as the Melonport.

11.3. A Basic, Newer Horizon

Undoubtedly, the confidence and adoption of cryptocurrencies can only be preserved if potential business players are willing to join quickly. Crypto wealth management solutions have a quick and more unified place for traders at all ability standards to handle their portfolios, and therefore a simpler route to joining the community.

The burgeoning investment class should begin to witness better development as these networks are becoming more popular and proceed to defrag the highly bifurcated crypto trading climate. Nevertheless, their effectiveness relies not only on having a central place to monitor investments but also as a platform to further comprehend the whole industry.

As organizations explore their shortcomings and find collaborators who can boost their market proposition, the next phase for wealth management solutions could be acquiring. The cryptocurrency industry would potentially open up to even greater exposure from the wider online trading ecosystem through developing and encouraging these extremely synergistic networks.

Chapter 12: How the Institutional Investors Sustain Cryptocurrency World?

They seemed to cater to tech-oriented buyers ready to gain a bit of a gamble since virtual currencies initially gained market interest. The virtual currency room of, say, 2015 seemed dangerous, a relatively untested market with plenty of concerns about legal status development opportunities, and more. Optimistic people may have wished for a breakthrough streak, such as the huge rise in values for cryptocurrencies that supposedly occurred late in 2016, but nobody knew it would occur. Unnecessary to mention, virtual currencies have not become an enticing opportunity to hold in mind for retail buyers and those with consumer preferences. Instead, the market spoke mostly to private buyers eager to take the gamble down the road for a future payout.

However, quick ahead to the latter several months of 2019, and the story seems very distinct. Although many virtual currencies are also staying solid, since the turning of the year, they have dropped considerably from their peak. Certain traders have fallen back to their expectations that virtual tokens can bring in a drastic and dramatic change in how the financial environment functions. At the same period, though, global investors are becoming more actively involved in technology, and they may have been more likely to persist in finding it in the future. Below, we would discuss how global investors have been interested and why cryptocurrencies have switched their attention.

12.1. The Institutional Investors Takes the Lead

As the biggest purchasers of virtual token bundles priced at more than $200,000 and by private sales, institutional investors outperformed high-net-worth individuals per Bloomberg, as per Cumberland's international head of trade, Bobby Cho.

Also, there are emerging goods, programs, transaction processes, and the latest participation among global investors. Bloomberg states that in many situations, traders have turned to professionalize their transaction modes, setting up daily coin transactions from their volatility desks and activities, although they might have traditionally waited for a price surge to offer stock of coins to the international platform.

All of this suggests that a digital currency that over the business has rocketed. As of April 2017, via CoinMarketCap, it protected up to $40 billion in transactions per day, relative to exchanges currently covered only $16 billion in trading every day. Around the same period, as opposed to the OTC sector, markets have witnessed their rates decline more dramatically from prior high levels in the virtual currency industry.

12.2. What Changed?

Why would retail investors unexpectedly opt to plunge into the room, most of whom were hesitant to consider a gamble on cryptos' only months earlier? A great deal of it will get down to liquidity. In the latest months, the virtual currency boom has calmed down. Cho states that "the industry has been dealing in a quite narrow range, and [this] appears to be associated with conventional financial entities becoming much more confident jumping into the room."

Personal purchases are a natural match for retail investors since major transactions that take place on platforms will move tokens' cost. Private sales empower transacting parties to set the cost ahead of schedule, taking out some of the complexity and danger. They often encourage broader trades that could be attractive to retail buyers, but on markets are more complicated to execute.

In current months as the prominence of virtual money among personal investors has decreased, financial firms have begun to engage in the sector for cryptocurrencies. Thinking ahead, and if these developments persist, they will wind up performing a key role in encouraging the sector's overall sustained development.

Chapter 13: What Is the Cryptocurrency Spoofing?

Severe uncertainty is among the cornerstones of most virtual currencies. Especially in the early stages of a few big cryptocurrencies, regular and critical price changes were a problem, but the trend persists to this day. You have to go no farther than the world's biggest virtual money, bitcoin (BTC), to see proof that it is the situation; BTC soared to the record peak of even more than $18,000 each coin in late 2018. It had fallen too far less than half of that amount just a couple of weeks later.

Cost variations spreading across months and weeks don't only exist on a broader time frame like this one. They even literally take effect from moment to second, too. This reality has helped certain illegal enterprises take advantage of common virtual currency flash drops, purchase the best tokens for lower rates, and instead sell them until the prices are fixed. Today, a recent development has generated fear for the cryptocurrency world as well. Named "fraud," it is the mechanism through which, by producing false orders, offenders aim to manipulate the cost of the virtual currency falsely.

13.1. A Spoofing Primer

The cost of a digital coin, like all tradable assets, depends on several variables, including the general feeling of hope or defeatism that pervades the broader economy and specific investors. Although it may be hard to measure this meaning of the cryptocurrency's strength and promise, it is nevertheless something that experienced investors are extremely receptive to. These ideas are crucial to the value of the coin, even though they appear somewhat obscure, because of the effect that a sense of hope or negativity may have on the propensity of a community of buyers to purchase or sell the virtual money.

This is the reality that such emotions are enigmatic, which makes it feasible and successful to spoof. By executing a fraudulent purchasing or selling request, traders attempting to exploit the demand for a specific cryptocurrency will produce the appearance of optimism or negativity. They manipulate other buyers into either purchasing or selling as traders create these demands without the purpose of satisfying them, and the value of a cryptocurrency faces the risk of being changed appropriately when the crypto-currency price shifts in the path they want, the dealer suspends the contracts.

13.2. Spoofing in the Practice

Bloomberg was commenting on a U.S. inquiry. The Department of Judiciary (DOJ) started to evaluate if, as a consequence of spoofing, blockchain market fixing has occurred throughout the bitcoin system. The DOJ authorities are worried because exchanges worldwide have adopted an aggressive path to targeting traders involved in spoofing, as per the paper. Bitcoin could be the probe's subject not just since it is the biggest virtual money by exchange value and also as its dramatic price spikes drove hundreds of fresh novice investors into existence late that year. Such buyers may have been the most vulnerable to spoofing, willing to create what they see to be simple money from digital money that appears bound for stratospheric peaks.

When the spoofing happens, it is sometimes followed by wiping. Wash trading appears close to tampering in how it attempts to influence the cost of digital money falsely, but the execution methods are distinct. A manipulative liar trades with itself in wash dealing with building the appearance of market requirement, thereby enticing naive buyers to join trades.

Prof. Griffin of finance at the University of Texas claims that the cryptocurrency room is especially vulnerable to spoofing. He describes that "there is hardly any surveillance of deceptive trading, tampering, and washes investing" in a cryptocurrency globe, contributing that hacking the industry and illegally tricking prices "would've been simple."

13.3. Guarding Against the Spoofing

How will the investor better defend themselves from trading in digital money when spoofing is occurring? Overall, for several buyers, vigilance is the key strategy. It is better to take note of possibilities that sound too nice to be real. Therefore, it is important to guarantee that all markets you transact on are cautious regarding the risk of theft of all sorts, like falsifying and washing. About the same time, in the attempt to defend against tampering and secure clients, several exchanges are trying to step up their encryption and surveillance programs.

For starters, the Gemini market, founded by Cameron and Tyler Winklevoss, currently unveiled a collaboration with NASDAQ to track digital token exchange.

Inevitably, even the most cautious buyers will also be vulnerable to market inflation in a digital money environment. It is also important to remember that this room stays extremely volatile and that virtual currencies may not just be the be-all and end-all of every investment policy.

Chapter 14: Why the Crypto Users require to Know ERC20 Standard?

Without a technological understanding of a blockchain and clever contract world, a cryptocurrency universe could have appeared overwhelming to the typical investor at one stage. Nevertheless, among all forms of consumers, particularly some who may otherwise have been careful about participating in a commodity or currency, the promise of large gains and the influx of several emerging digital currencies has attracted the internal workings of all that they may not grasp clearly. While investors will be effective in a cryptocurrency room without such technological expertise, a clear knowledge of several of the most critical attributes of several of the new digital assets is undeniably helpful in leading the investor into the easiest and soundest financial choices. The ERC20 token norm is among the main principles that regulate a significant part of the area.

ERC20 applies to Ethereum as a coin standard. This is a technical specification that specifies a set of laws and acts which must be worthy of being executed by an Ethereum coin or smarter contract. The ERC represents the "Ethereum demand for information, and in 2016 the norm was created.'Request for information' is a variant of a related concept introduced by the Web Engineering Tasks Force as a way of sharing critical technological notes and specifications. Maybe it is better to think about ERC20 as a series of simple instructions and features that should be followed by every new token generated in the Ethereum system.

14.1. The Prevalence and the Importance of ERC20

For some period, the ERC20 norm has been a prominent direction for developing new currencies in a virtual currency space. For ICOs and crowdfunding firms, this has been especially successful. Through certain estimates, as of the very first weeks of 2018, there have been more than 30,000 separate tokens running according to the ERC20 format. A Yahoo! News article indicates the ERC20 coins "perhaps single-handedly controlled the ICO market crash of 2018" and that several popular cryptocurrencies are developed as per the ERC20 method. EOS is the most popular token built on ERC20 as of the writing, despite earning $195 million in the five days ICO release. Next on the chart, Bancor is raised during the selling of $154 million in equity crowdfunding. Several other ERC20 tractable tokens in ICOs already collected at least $80 million individually.

14.2. History of ERC20

The ERC20 was established on the part of the larger Ethereum system and ecosystem by Ethereum developers in 2016 and formally recognized in September 2016. The developer or community of developers should apply what has been recognized as the Ethereum Enhancement Proposal (EIP) with unique methods and specifications to establish a specification of this kind for Ethereum. The committee instead accepts amends and finalizes the EIP, which constitutes an ERC at that stage.

Good contracts will then be required to meet all of the requirements. Among all the ERC norms, ERC20 has been the better established, but it is not the least one that exists.

14.3. The Contents of ERC20 Standard

There are many features in ERC20, which implies that a compatible token should be sufficient to enforce the checklist (the details of each feature are in brackets):

Total Supply Obtained (provide info about a total coin

supply)

The Balance of (Should provide credit balance of the holder)

The transfer (start executing the transfer of a given number of coins to a designated location)

The Transferring From (start execute the transfer of the given number of coins from the specified location)

The Authorize (allowing the spender to withdraw the fixed number of coins from a particular account)

Allowance (come back to the purchaser of a fixed number of coins from the spender). In fact, up to two activities can also be caused by these features, such as the transfer activity (which happens once tokens are relocated) and the authorization event initiated when approval is requested.

In March 2017, Coinbase revealed its intention to introduce assistance for ERC20 to a variety of all its products. According to Yahoo! Media, this move's introduction is supposed to "launch up the gates for a much more inclusive set of cryptocurrency transactions" on the Coinbase Custody platform.2 As per Yahoo! News, platforms belonging to personal investors may also incorporate additional commodities to the Coinbase Custody system.

14.4. Issues and their Alternatives

Although ERC20 has seen tremendous help in the shape of tokens that adhere to its specifications, those who claim ERC20 are deficient in one or maybe more respect in the creative world. For this purpose, a variety of alternate token specifications also have been suggested after the evolution of ERC20. This included ERC223, which seeks to resolve a problem with the acceptance and transition aspects of ERC20.5 Another solution is ERC621, which proposes the same core functions offered by ERC20. Still, it also introduces the potential to raise or reduce the overall availability of tokens.6 but on the other side, ERC827 enables the owner to accept the expenditure of coins by the third entity.

Chapter 15: The Cryptocurrency 'Burning': Is it able to handle Inflation?

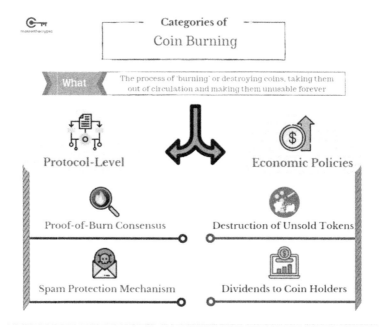

Virtual currencies grew to popularity in both the national news and market interest over the last year and a half. There are still several famous holdouts, but many more buyers are buying the significance of digital currency and cryptocurrency technologies. Consequently, the combined valuation of all the cryptocurrencies grew by over 4,000 percent in about 12 months. A reality that certain developers could get very rich from the fashionable modern investment region quite rapidly has only fueled more excitement in the city. Nevertheless, there will be some patterns that have arrived and gone except in the limited period in which virtual currencies also caught our interest. One of the first big developments in a cryptocurrency room was Bitcoin; soon afterward, anonymity coins such as Dash and the Monero appeared to be a rave. Today, another practice appears to have been one of the top trending aspects of the field of virtual currencies: coin consuming.

"Burning" a coin relates to the transfer of the otherwise available coin (or proportion thereof) to the inaccessible account in the context of cryptocurrencies.

Appropriately, the action of burning eliminates coins from the stock available, raising their comparative scarcity.

The Proof-of-burn (the PoB) was the agreement process that is used to protect and verify a blockchain framework that depends on the charred principle and is perceived as a tool that is quite cost-effective than common substitutes.

15.1. What Is the Coin Burning?

The idea of "coin consuming" brings back visions of the investor matching a physical currency. Of course, it is not feasible because virtual currencies function only in digital form. Fortunately, the principle is the one that holds. As per Motley Fool, coin incineration is the mechanism by which virtual money miners and creators may withdraw tokens or assets from distribution, thus decelerating the rate of inflation or decreasing the overall distributed number of coins.

How can this be achieved? It is challenging, if not impractical, in the virtual currency environment to monitor tokens' movement until they can be created. Miners and investors purchase such coins to eliminate coins from distribution, and then give them to unique domains that have unachievable personal keys. Nobody may use these coins without control to a secret key for the reasons of employing them for purchases. Thus, the tokens become inaccessible and are confined to the space beyond the circulation supply for all the intents and objectives.

15.2. The Background of the Coin Burning

The Cryptocurrencies was not the one to explore the idea of coin burning. In reality, this method is very analogous to purchasing back shares from a commonly listed corporation. Organizations of this sort utilize money on hand to purchase away common shares securities, thus decreasing the remaining overall shares. This mechanism aims to strengthen the liquidity of certain securities that stay in trading and will also tend to boost profits per share. The value of total profits to assets gets greater with fewer remaining shares.

The Coin burning attempts to achieve a common purpose. Creators and miners aim to create the coins that stay in circulation tougher, and therefore more expensive, by lowering the number of tokens in demand.

15.3. The Proof-of-Burn

The Proof of Burn (PoB) is one of the many agreement protocol algorithms introduced by a blockchain system to guarantee that the real and correct state is accepted between all involved nodes. A POW device without power loss is sometimes referred to as a POB. It works on the concept of empowering users to "burn" tokens for virtual currencies. The privilege to compose blocks following the burned coins is therefore given to them.

To explain the algorithm, the POB method creator, Iain Stewart, employs an analogy burnt tokens are like logging rigs. A miner consumes their tokens to purchase simulated mining equipment in this metaphor, which allows them to mine the blocks. More and more money burnt by a miner, the greater the "rig" for simulated mining would be.

Miners dispatch them to a provably un-spendable location to consume the coins. This method (besides the burnt coins) does not take much energy and means that the system stays productive and scalable. Miners are permitted to consume the indigenous currency or the money of an analogous chain, like Bitcoin, depending on the execution. In return, they earn a payout from the blockchain's indigenous currency coin.

You will submit transfers that would burn the own crypto-currency coins to the system. At the highest point of the block, other stakeholders may mine/burn, and they may even take other respondents' transactions to link these to the block. Most of this burning action effectively makes the network active, and users are paid for their operations (both consuming their assets and consuming the money of many other individuals).

The POB scheme has introduced a process that encourages the intermittent burning of blockchain tokens to retain mining capacity to eliminate the risk of disproportionate benefits for early investors. Any time the new block is produced, the strength of burnt assets "decays" or decreases slightly. Rather than a one-time, initial expenditure, this facilitates daily action by miners. To retain a sustainable advantage as technology progresses, miners will need to invest in improved machinery regularly.

15.4. The Practical Applications of the Coin Burning

At least two crypto currencies have indeed managed to melt coins. Bitcoin money has dramatically increased in value getting into the season.

The Cryptocurrency mining club Antpool revealed on April 20 that it had submitted 12percent of the bitcoin money coins it collects to unachievable accounts as block incentives for verifying transactions. This is not a tiny volume of money, given that Antpool affirms anywhere similar to 10 percent of bitcoin money transactions. Consequently, Antpool is decelerating the rate of inflation for the BCH, which could lead to the huge rise of bitcoin cash in recent times.

However, Binance Coin (BNB) tested this technique until bitcoin money ended up getting in on token burning. BNB seems to be the authorized token of the virtual currency trading of Binance; BNB is being used to encourage consumers, encouraging them to pay phased transaction costs. 9About 1. Million BNB coins were burnt during the first several weeks of each year, according to estimates. In April, with yet another $40 million or more of BNB burnt at the point, the method was replicated. BNB was about to witness the same huge improvements seen by bitcoin money until now, yet so far, the whole year, it has become a good performer of virtual currencies.

There have been huge dangers involved with money burning, for instance, too. Second, there is no certainty that the existing coins would increase in worth from consuming coins. The cumulative number of tokens remaining in circulation may not even decline since the availability of coins in circulation tends to vary tremendously.

An illustration of why money burning could not operate is Bitcoin. Bitcoin has a maximum of 22 million coins; some experts claim that this restriction continues to add to BTC's appeal. Nevertheless, due to the so-called "strong forks." Bitcoin has indeed produced new forms of currencies in some ways. And that is how bitcoin money, the bitcoin gold, and other altcoins, for instance, come to be. And in the future, many more assets will be produced if Bitcoin were ever to branch further.

Nevertheless, it is necessary to remember that although new coins are normally given to owners of the initial token through the forking phase, the freshly released token retains its independent blockchain, and the current tokens not equivalent to the existing ones. Thus, despite separate protocols, economies, and consumer groups, cryptocurrency and bitcoin money are two completely different ventures.

Chapter 16: How Cryptocurrencies Impact the Estate Planning?

Estate strategy has often become very difficult for investment accounts, but it has been considerably more so than in the age of virtual currencies. It seemed that shareholders should carry out the will and provide things such as share certificates for attorney kin's power in a secure place and that the asset transfer would go seamlessly. Today, if the investor wishes to make confident that their digital properties are securely and efficiently moved whenever the time arrives, some modern rules and guidelines must be followed.

Down, when it refers to online properties, we'll discuss a few of the pros and downs of estate management. The laws have not been modified in certain situations. There are unique aspects to bear in consideration that conventional investors might not have been informed of in other situations.

16.1. The secret to information and access

When estate management for cryptocurrency, maybe the sole most critical aspect is knowing that the estate's executor understands which properties you possess and how you would reach them. A new Forbes study reveals that acquiring these properties would be the most daunting part of the operation.

Investors with cryptocurrencies are pretty unpredictable regarding how their cryptographic keys and authorization codes are stored. Because these codes enable complete accessibility to digital accounts, this is baffling. Be too careful, on the other side, with stuff, and you face the danger of missing the key. There is always no means to restore control if this occurs, and the wallet loaded with crypto tokens will go indefinitely unused.

An ancient technique: "I'm the massive supporter of pen and paper," for naming cryptocurrency codes for trustees and heirs, is suggested by Crypto asset succession planning specialist Pam Morgan. Morgan continues that "this is most essential to illustrate [to them] the types of resources, key, the locations, and control mechanisms you're using for safety. Accessing controls are items like PINs, the passphrases, the multi-signature or time-lock specifications."

16.2. The Ethical Part of Situations

Nevertheless, with a straightforward description of where the digital currencies are and how the descendants will reach them if they do not take appropriate measures, you may set the immediate family for trouble with the law. Preferably, that investors would regard both technological usability and ethical implications. Shareholders may establish their descendants for protracted litigation without addressing the legal questions involved with financial planning. On the other side, Morgan admits, "excluding [crypto] keys, the court order is powerless."

Morgan advises that they make at least three versions of asset documents and archive them in different places. This list, especially for extremely active crypto-currency traders, could be useful in reviewing as much as once a week. On the other side, the cryptocurrency estate management specialist, Chicago lawyer Michael Goldberg, indicates that investors who are already occasionally involved may potentially move away with fewer wealth portfolios. I have a reasonably broad selection [of tokens], "I have such a fairly diverse range [of tokens],"

From a constitutional point of view in recent years, several states have passed regulations enabling attorneys to handle intangible assets comparably to how conventional resources could be handled. This may benefit if executors need to auction off block-chain resources immediately; as the digital coins decline in cost in the process, this will protect them from experiencing the outcry from descendants. Nevertheless, although the legislation is rushing to keep up with crypto property management, there still is space for progress. President Tamara Curry of the National College of Probate Judge says that lawyers and judges would have to get more versed in cryptocurrency. Courts will be likely to be more deluged. Lawyers are supposed to be trained and kept informed about what to search for whenever these resources appear before judges," said Curry.

Chapter 17: Cryptocurrency trends

It is still interesting to forecast the future of the crypto sector, but due to, and as compared to, the conventional financing structure, it is concurrently evolving. On the other side, the adoption of crypto user identity criteria, the increasing surge in virtual government currency the PayPal cryptosystem, and the imminent release of the stable coin, the Diem (ex-Libra), via Facebook, and several other activities indicate that digital resources are finally becoming more understandable and more widespread.

17.1. Which type of coins rise and which ones fall in price?

On the other side, the pace of delivery of cryptocurrencies relies specifically on how easily transactions become accessible and approved in each conventional bank or transaction mechanism with their different products and varieties. The widespread usage of intangible properties is something the planet is seeking to do and what it expects. It is the effort to establish an equilibrium in using cryptocurrencies between advantage and danger that will decide 2021 patterns.

Trend One: Tax enforcement to be used by Crypto.

The tax enforcement of cryptocurrencies is the principal issue for the foreseeable future. Crypto taxing is indeed a mysterious thing today, an abstract image far removed from the truth. Crypto taxation is still not universal, even although they are undesirable to others. When those industries grow, and policymakers recognize their money generating value outweighing past crypto risks, they also started emerging in some nations.

The implementation of compulsory user authentication by Know the Customer (KYC) protocols, the creation of specifications that allow monitoring transactions, and an acceptance of virtual currency regulations, however, obviously demonstrate that trends are evolving and growing quicker than some would anticipate.

We often witness the successful creation of surveillance software, together with authorities sharing details on cryptocurrency investors and the purchases they are creating. Thus, the planet is expected to encounter the very first bitcoin taxation avoidance litigation in 2021.

Trend Two: There are "Distant Crypto Harbors" mostly on the way.

The adoption of crypto taxes would improve the appeal of regimes that would oppose this activity since there exists an anti-trend with any trend and encourage consumers to reduce the expense of possessing digital wealth legitimately. The so-called' overseas crypto reserves' can grow more aggressively, to put it. The economies whereby IT and the capital market both are better known would most definitely perform this position, such as Thailand, Korea, Singapore, and Switzerland.

Trend Three: The very first problem in cryptography is heading.

Not merely is the progressing field of cryptography becoming much more open, controlled, and protected, it is also starting to face a variety of economic hurdles and evaluations. We are now witnessing the harbingers of the first cybercrime or fraud epidemic, which has nothing to do with it.

The value of Bitcoin (BTC) reached a fresh milestone in December, hitting the $35,000 mark. Nevertheless, the explanation was not just the increasing market for BTC and an excessive supply of the stable coins Tether (USDT) on the platform, which is utilized to perform 70% of crypto trading platforms.

The Tether, which is documented in the British Virgin Areas, is increasingly growing its pollution to boost its money's profitability. At the same period, market participants have severe concerns that USDT coins are genuinely funded by fiat money, i.e., US currency. In turn, Tether is operated by the iFinex group, for which plaintiffs brought a $1.5 trillion class interest case in 2017-2018 on allegations of business fraud.

Consequently, what we experience now on crypto markets is what occurs when policymakers in the conventional economies set up printing presses: the surplus availability of fiat currency in the system contributes to the accumulation of assets and hence their drop in value. We observe the deflation of capital, which is presently USDT in the cryptocurrency market, which contributes to an improvement in the price of BTC products in the crypto environment. Present patterns will also contribute to more deflation in altcoins and the rise in bitcoin rates, the emissions of which are fully established to be restricted.

Trend four: Models for risk analysis will strengthen.

And against the backdrop of the increase in bitcoin's worth, the beginnings of a large risk evaluation model are urgently needed. It is becoming extremely challenging for users to accurately evaluate crypto investments' potential outcomes without falling victim to the overall rush. Systems that provide a working remedy would be able to immediately rule the hearts, brains, and pockets of both novices and qualified members in the cryptocurrency industry, not just "virtual fortune advising on the coffee basis.

There have been over 9,000 distinct crypto commodities in the globe today, as per Coin Market Cap. And over 80% of them, as they can be called in the market, are dishonest schemes or 'frauds.' Several of the surviving 20%, even so, show productivity rates that are no weaker, and even sometimes greater, than the Bitcoin.

At the same time, a wide range of consequences that could increase or crash the significance of a particular currency must be considered by those who are planning to spend in crypto:

Organizational: for instance, the country in which the authorizing company as well as the crypto transfer function and regulatory changes occurring in that region, besides or against virtual currencies.

Strategic: code inaccuracies, weak data security, and feeble data security, most of which could even be used to grab cryptocurrencies by malicious hackers.

Value risks: a most problematic to evaluate is still this level of risk. Even so, cheers to the widespread regulations of KYC (user verification) and KYT (payment identification); experts are willing to monitor large portions of cryptocurrencies' mobility and evaluate who does own them and monitor their sales-related decisions. Depending on the objectives, time, and other features of such sales, it is conceivable to produce assumptions about alterations in the worth of a cryptocurrency that relied on the information acquired. It also tends to make the spike in the magnitude of the industry less reliant on personal supposition.

Today, there will be less ambiguity in the crypto globe, and more options are available to create analytical techniques. The complexities of substitute finance, even so, are still challenging for newbie investors to comprehend.

Services that provide a workable solution would rapidly overcome the hearts, brains, and pockets of both newcomers and accomplished contributors in the cryptocurrency industry, not just' electronic money mostly on beans leaves and the coffee grounds.'

Trend five: It could change the price of payments.

This trend, in that it would be multifactorial, is fascinating. Due to technological improvements, ether payments would become affordable, or Bitcoin transfers would increase in market value.

Modifications in operating costs can affect performers in an e-commerce market's benefit in cryptocurrencies. Its acquisition of crypto nowadays draws online shops because it is far affordable to engage with it than fiat commodities. As a transaction method, the pace of the crypto's propagation will primarily evaluate if it is sufficient to keep this benefit in a long-time frame.

Trend six: 5G is trying to redefine a number and improve a lot.

A modern concept of data processing, which is also misunderstood by so many, has been the 5G norm. Its introduction would contribute to introducing novel technologies and forms of resources and will impact the construction of processing, Defi software production, and much more.

With 5G, the features of transaction processing can no further be confined to system data rates. For instance, where machines take investment judgments, 5G will dramatically alter the high trading category, particularly with the ultra-low synchronization provided by 5G.

Traders today fail to position their server as near the crypto exchange because the wire duration influences how easily they may place or remove an order. 5G would help solve this barrier: all networks, irrespective of where a crypto transaction is situated, would have a fair playing ground for purchases.

What is going on in front of our site is what, till now, critics felt was inconceivable: the field of investment has been globalized. Regulators, conventional financial firms, and crypto businesses are gradually working together to allow the best of the advantages that have been provided to the planet by crypto technologies. While not all big problems have been answered currently, I am confident that in 2021 we would have solutions to most of them. A good result is completely unavoidable as crypto begins to evolve into broad global adoption.

Chapter 18: 5 Countries that have Banned Cryptocurrencies

Uncertainty appears to be brought on by the field of cryptocurrency. Some policymakers have posed concerns regarding their existence, while some are proposing national virtual money.

Cryptocurrencies are autonomous, ensuring that the respective central institutions or national banks in separate countries do not control them. Therefore, legislatures across the globe are introducing laws about regulating them, with the absence of a unified method to regulate them.

Any government laws enable cryptocurrency trading and transfers, while others have agreed that it is better to prohibit them entirely.

18.1. How have certain countries accepted cryptocurrencies?

The Cryptocurrencies may be exchanged, processed, or used in several nations across the world, like Singapore, South Korea, Germany, and Switzerland, in addition to the United States.

Bitcoin has been used for over ten years already and is the largest of cryptocurrencies. A Japanese govt heartily welcomed it from the beginning. Japan also generated special laws, and bitcoin, the biggest industry share, retains over 70 percent of the national money.

Bitcoin's second-largest industry value is kept in US currencies, and the market has multiple blockchain firms in the U.S.

While cryptocurrencies are not deemed lawful tender by the German authorities, they may be utilized as a money replacement. Bitcoin and similar cryptocurrencies are permitted for exchange and trade.

Cryptocurrencies are classified as fixed resources (assets) in several nations, like Australia, and are prone to Capital

18.2. Where are the cryptocurrencies not considered legal?

Several nations also deem cryptocurrencies unconstitutional and either have outlawed them or who have trade and usage limits.

There are the four most prominent nations in which cryptocurrencies have also been prohibited or rendered outright unlawful:

1. China first permitted trading in cryptocurrencies

Formerly, China was host to several exchanges in cryptocurrencies. Becoming the globe's more populous nation, they were tall. Cryptocurrencies in 2016, nevertheless, were prohibited. Ever since, for greater accountability and transaction monitoring, the Chinese regulators also implemented cryptocurrency technologies into the financial entities.

Currently, 90% of cryptocurrency development is believed to exist in China owing to its affordable capital. Allegations seem to be that China is preparing to outlaw mining and is planning to introduce a nationwide cryptocurrency. Some assume that this might soon proceed to China removing its cryptocurrency prohibition.

2. Bolivia aims to restrict the usage of crypto currencies.

Due to escalated criminal operations within the government, Bolivia is hesitant to permit cryptocurrencies. A secret pyramid plan including shares in cryptocurrencies was also just discovered and denounced. This triggered a declaration by Bolivia's National Bank restating that the nation is forbidden from using cryptocurrencies.

3. Colombia suspects illegal operations.

It's indeed unlawful to run cryptocurrency in Colombia, although this is one of Latin America's major FinTech markets. If they illegally manage bitcoins, several firms fear losing ties to financial resources. Even so, several emerging ventures concentrate on bitcoin and cryptocurrency and therefore are confronting an unpredictable future.

There has been one latest effort in 2017 to control the sector, but the Colombian Senate dismissed the plan. The idea would be for cryptocurrency to create a 5 percent tax on every sale, but what politicians seem to care about more are concerns of illegal activity and pyramid strategies.

4. Russia aims to prohibit the issuance and distribution of cryptocurrency.

So far, dealing in cryptocurrencies in Russia is partially legitimate, just not to purchase products and resources. Russia is due to introduce a virtual currency bill shortly and intends to approve a moratorium on the issuance and distribution of cryptocurrency. As Per an article in Forbes, the officials in Russia concern about the economic uncertainty virtual currencies will trigger. They claim that the safety of customers is important, as is a need to stop currency laundering.

5. Cryptocurrencies have been legally outlawed by Iran.

The usage of cryptocurrency in purchases was prohibited by the Iranian National Bank a while ago. Money smuggling and extremism became their greatest concerns, but it was still introduced as a strategy to monitor the collapse of their increasingly devaluing currency.

Chapter 19: Frequently asked questions

What is the gap between crypto-currency and virtual money?

The distinction between such virtual money and a blockchain is that the other remains decentralized, implying that a central body such as the national bank or state does not regulate or endorse it. Cryptocurrencies, instead, exist through a computing network. Digital assets already have the functionality of standard currencies, but they still work in the electronic environment. A central government is releasing them.

How many various forms of wallets are there for crypto currency?

There are five major categories of wallets for cryptocurrencies, namely desktop wallets, smartphone wallets, online wallets, wallets for hardware, and wallets for paper. If you are selling cryptocurrencies with a CFD account, you do not need a wallet, only while you are purchasing them. Cryptocurrencies are used for saving, submitting, and accepting wallets.

What type of cryptocurrency was the first one?

Bitcoin became the first cryptocurrency. In 2009, the bitcoin name was licensed, but the very initial transaction happened in 2010. Someone nicknamed 'Satoshi Nakamoto' invented it. There is evidence that Nakamoto is a nickname since the founder of bitcoin is famously anonymous and that no one recognizes if 'he' is an individual or a party.

Cryptocurrency is actual money, right?

An option for real money is cryptocurrency. Nowadays, some sources recognize cryptocurrency as a means of transaction. Nevertheless, since they are subjective and highly unpredictable, they show no similarity to other investment types. They are primarily used for theorizing on increases and drops in value among traders.

How many more cryptocurrencies seem to be there?

Although several have no worth, there are about 2000 cryptocurrencies free to purchase and sell. Of all these, the highest influential market capitalization is bitcoin, the ether (the Ethereum system) ripple, bitcoin money (an outgrowth of bitcoin), and the bitcoin.

IG provides trade on nine of the most popular cryptocurrencies: the bitcoin, bitcoin money, cryptocurrency gold, ether, the ripple, Litecoin, the EOS, the stellar (XLM), and a NEO.

What is the right moment for crypto-currency trading?

The demand for cryptocurrencies runs 24 hours per day, seven days each week, ensuring there has been no perfect time to sell as demand fluctuations can occur at any moment. And since cryptos have been exchanged internationally, the various time ranges imply that the business will still be busy everywhere.

While exchanging provides more possibilities for exchange around the hour, it also renders it necessary to have danger control instruments. You have ease of mind when you seem to be not always around the track of the business.

Cryptocurrencies seem to be open for trading with IG every time between 4 am on Sunday to 10 pm on Monday (UK time).

What has pushed the demand for cryptocurrencies?

This crypto-currency industry is, like other economies, guided by the powers of supplies and consumption. The production and usage of cryptocurrencies can be affected by a range of variables, including:

- News.

- Fear of the market

- Politics and the control of the government

- Technical advancement

- The wellbeing of fiat money

Why can IG earn profit by investing in cryptocurrencies?

Our trading algorithm searches through several exchanges and extracts a rational mid-price, applying a range of points to each hand, regarded as the offset, to generate the cost we post on the website. Because of the propagation, until you are also in benefit, the place has to travel a specific distance, and this is our trading charge. If you choose to leave the place active overnight, you'd still have to pay the bill.

Conclusion

In the international financial environment, crypto currencies are indeed a popular subject. Crypto coin exchange prices are extremely unpredictable. There seems to be a strong chance of selling these cryptocurrencies with this. Their rise has also been capable of attracting several speculators' interest. They are comfortably compact. After the requisite confidence in the cryptocurrencies, they can be seen on a larger scale afterward. If cryptocurrencies do not acquire that confidence, then their boost can diminish. They are only in their adolescence, and it is not known that they can be exchanged internationally to maturity in the industries. Several various cryptocurrencies have received the needed interest. Some countries have begun to issue domestic cryptocurrencies. It is also likely that bitcoins will eventually have a route to grow with cryptocurrencies. In terms of the limilations, bitcoins in the digital economy are nevertheless called tour-de-force. This has supported the least developing countries with an alternate currency and has unlocked the path of global change. In either way, more options are offered to consumers to handle their finances. Despite the reference to the lofty transitions carried out by bitcoins, cryptocurrencies are viewed to reach the financial level and forever alter the international financial landscape. Cryptocurrencies include many internal problems to tackle in parallel to fighting the global economic structure. For starters, seeking to transform the entire global financial structure to the Bitcoin paradigm might trigger such large blockchain size development that the dispersed ledger model will become unrealistic. A cryptocurrency that strives to be a component of the conventional financial structure would have to follow broadly divergent specifications. It will have to be numerically abstract (to deter theft and intruder attacks) but simple to comprehend for customers; decentralized but with sufficient security and protection for customers; and maintaining consumer privacy without becoming a platform for tax avoidance, money smuggling, and other illegal practices. Is it conceivable that even the most common cryptocurrency in the next few years will have characteristics that fell between highly controlled paper money and today's cryptocurrencies because these are enormous requirements to meet? If the probability seems distant, there is no question that the performance (or absence thereof) of Bitcoin in grappling with the difficulties it confronts as the main cryptocurrency at current will decide the fate of many cryptocurrencies in the coming years. Like anything else in existence, Crypto could be both positive and bad. Most individuals struggle to grasp cryptocurrencies' true meaning, so they're just based on commodity investing guided by price and uncertainty.

Crypto has a special strategy that leaves fiat money redundant. Cryptocurrency allows individuals to become their independent bank and means of payment. The Regulatory and technological problems are the major ones. User-adoption seems to be the determining variable on which crypto replaces currency. Yet blockchain can render the future appear unique until it is mounted and incorporated into our lives, in respects we could only start to grasp.

Now that you have heard more about cryptocurrencies, their advantages, problems, operating, and other information. We assume that as you reach the field of cryptocurrencies and investing, this book would be a fantastic guide for you.

Printed in Great Britain
by Amazon

68859534R10098